READY OR NOT, HERE I COME!

ALLEN COLE

Published by Allen Cole

Ready or Not, Here I Come!

© COPYRIGHT 2021 by Allen Cole

All Rights Reserved

ISBN: 978-1-7369630-0-5 (Paperback edition)

978-1-7369630-1-2 (eBook edition)

PREFACE

In looking around for information in how to prepare the End Times and the Second Coming, I only found mostly superficial ideas. Most books were concerned about the who, the what, when and the how about these events, the more important issue of personal preparation was mostly missing. This was puzzling since Jesus talked so much about His return and warned us and challenged us to be ready and prepared. But how to be ready and prepared well becomes the challenge.

The purpose for writing this book, "Ready or Not Here I Come!" is so that the true and sincere believers are able to properly prepare their hearts.

It is my plan to write three short books on this topic of the End Times and the Second Coming. The first book, I would consider the most important of the three because it places the focus on preparation. Knowing the what and the when will not be beneficial, if one is not spiritually, mentally, emotionally, and relationally prepared for the events leading up to Second Coming.

The second and third books will discuss more the what and the when, but again they are secondary in importance to this first book.

The book, "Ready or Not Here I Come!" will not be the nice curl-up-on-the-couch-in-front-of-the-fireplace book. This is a study book meant to provoke you, challenge you, and cause you to reflect deeply on how you are currently living your life. It will ask hard questions. The tendency is to often dismiss such questions, ignore them altogether, or you may even find the book to be offensive in its probing. Please do not allow any of these things to happen.

This book is not meant to be a quick read, after which you move on to the next thing. As we move closer to the end of the age, the events happening on and to the earth will be terrifying. Our comfort and encouragement must come from the Lord of heaven and earth. Things will not become easier. If we are alert and prepared for what is to come, then no matter what happens, things will be much better for us in the end.

It is important to explain what this book will not suggest to you. This book will not tell that you to sell all you have and move out into the jungle or a desert place. You should not abandon your station in life and just go hide out someplace.

In the book of Luke, Jesus tells a parable, and He makes quite an interesting statement about how we should conduct ourselves.

Luke 19:11-14 {11} While they were listening to these things, Jesus went on to tell a parable, because He was near Jerusalem, and they supposed that the kingdom of God was going to appear immediately. 12 So He said, "A nobleman went to a distant country to receive a kingdom for himself, and then return. 13 "And he called ten of his slaves, and gave them ten minas and said to them, 'Do business with this until I come back.' (NASU)

Jesus tells His servants to busy themselves with business or trade. Now, obviously, the primary thought or idea is to be busy about the work of the kingdom of God, but there is also the thought that we are to live our lives by being responsible and making a living.

What makes this so difficult is that we often have the wrong values and priorities to begin with, so we think that throwing off responsibility and going to the mountains is the best solution. Or we dismiss the idea of a near Second Coming as craziness and change nothing. Both are a travesty. So how should we live in this tension?

One day I was talking to a man about this topic and he said to me, "I cannot think of anything that I would change in how I am living right now." It was a great shock, and I felt such sadness at the same time. We all have things that need adjusting and to be reprioritized. To not be able to see these things does not help in preparation.

Consider the questions listed below, which will challenge us how to be responsible in this life while at the same time considering the nearness of Christ's Coming.

• Do I seek God's kingdom first, more than anything else?

• Are the things that are eternal have the most value in my life?

• Is there an eternal perspective in all the decisions I am making?

• Are all my attitudes godly and God honoring?

• Have I developed a tolerance for sin in my life?

• Is my thinking in alignment with God's thinking (i.e., the Bible)?

- Am I struggling with negative emotions and feelings?

- Are all my relationships in good order and pleasing to the Lord?

- Are my plans held loosely, and given to God?

- Am I properly dealing with idolatries and sexual immoralities in my life? If not, am I making progress in eliminating and overcoming these types of sins, as these sins are the most dangerous to us as humans?

- Do I have a good theology of suffering? Am I really willing to suffer loss for the sake of Christ, or could I end up compromising? Have I already compromised? Am I daily taking up the cross of Christ?

- Do I fear God as the Bible defines the fear of God?

- Are my finances God honoring and kingdom orientated? Do I have debt?

Do you notice what questions are missing above? The typical questions that invariably arise when we discuss the topic of our Lord's return are:

- "Should I get married?" Absolutely

- "Should I continue with my educational plans?" Absolutely

- "Should we have children?" Absolutely

- "Should I quit my job?" Absolutely not!

- "Should I move to the mountains or the desert?" Absolutely not!

- "Should I sell everything?" Only if God has specifically told you to do so.

If we are managing the first list correctly, then the last group of questions should be moot points.

ONE

INTRODUCTION

"This gospel of the kingdom shall be preached in the whole world as a testimony to all the nations, and then the end will come."

Why this book and why now? What I am about to say will both excite you and cause you to pause and give serious contemplation about the End Times and the Second Coming.

My wife and I have been working on a UUPG (Unreached, Unengaged People Groups) project for nearly three years now, and it has been a great blessing. For those who do not know what UUPGs are, they are people groups who have never heard about Jesus or they are people groups who may have heard, but there are only just a few, or one or two, within that people group who have made a commitment to Christ.

Currently, we are working in a country that is not at all friendly to the gospel, but instead is quite antagonistic. One of the great motivating factors for engaging in this ministry at nearly retirement age was the verse in Matthew 24:14, which says, "This gospel of the kingdom shall be preached in the whole world as a testimony to all the nations, and then the end will come.[1]

This was a great opportunity for us to engage in a ministry the Bible says is directly connected to the Second Coming of Christ. Of course, my wife and I could not say 'no'. So, we sold off or gave away almost everything we owned and joined the project.

Recently, around September of 2020, the leader of the project we are working on was speaking to some men who are responsible for raising funds for ministries that are engaging these last few UUPGs around the world. They told the leader of the project at the rate we are currently going; WE WILL REACH ALL OF THE UUPGs WORLDWIDE BY THE END OF 2022.

Did you just read that last sentence? Let those words penetrate deeply into your minds and hearts. Think about what Jesus said to us in Matthew. Do you understand the implications of what this means? It means that the end is close, very close!

The world is not going to end in 2022, as there are just too many other things that need to happen that have not yet happened. God's list and our human lists are not the same, meaning there would be a bit more work to do after we finish our existing list. More than likely, we will discover groups we missed previously. But what this does mean is that the church is closer than ever in fulfilling the mandate of preaching the gospel to the ends of the earth.

This verse in Matthew is the greatest biblical marker that has been given to us directly by Jesus to indicate that the all the history of the human race is nearing the end.

This is the reason for this book!

While I was ecstatic about this news, a new reality begun to sink in; and it caused me to reflect deeply about my own personal life. It forced me to ask the hard question, "Am I personally ready for all that is about to happen?"

Wow! What a thought, what an idea. This hard question requires an equally honest answer. As we look at our lives, are we truly prepared as we should be? Could there be some areas of our lives where there is some urgent personal work still needing to be done in order to be properly prepared?

Paul, in his first letter to the Thessalonians tells them to both comfort, encourage, and build up one another concerning the resurrection of the saints and the Second Coming of Christ.

1 Thessalonians 4:13-18 {13} But we do not want you to be uninformed, brethren, about those who are asleep, so that you will not grieve as do the rest who have no hope. 14 For if we believe that Jesus died and rose again, even so God will bring with Him those who have fallen asleep in Jesus. 15 For this we say to you by the word of the Lord, that we who are alive and remain until the coming of the Lord, will not precede those who have fallen asleep. 16 For the Lord Himself will descend from heaven with a shout, with the voice of the archangel and with the trumpet of God, and the dead in Christ will rise first. 17 Then we who are alive and remain will be caught up together with them in the clouds to meet the Lord in the air, and so we shall always be with the Lord. 18 Therefore **comfort one another** with these words. (NASU)

1 Thessalonians 5:1-11 {1} Now as to the times and the epochs, brethren, you have no need of anything to be written to you. 2 For you yourselves know full well that the day of the Lord will come just like a thief in the night. 3 While they are saying, "Peace and safety!" then destruction will come upon them suddenly like labor pains upon a woman with child, and they will not escape. 4 But you, brethren, are not in darkness, that the day would overtake you like a thief; 5 for you are all sons of light and sons of day. We are not of night nor of darkness; 6 so then let us not sleep as others do but let us be alert and sober. 7 For those who sleep do their sleeping at night, and those who get drunk get drunk at night. 8 But since we are of the day, let us be sober, having put on the breastplate of faith and love, and as a helmet, the hope of salvation. 9 For God has not destined us for wrath, but

for obtaining salvation through our Lord Jesus Christ, 10 who died for us, so that whether we are awake or asleep, we will live together with Him. 11 Therefore **encourage one another** and **build up one another**, just as you also are doing. (NASU)

It is with great hope that not only are you challenged, but that the pages of this study book will comfort, encourage, and build you up to be all you can be in Christ. In this manner, you will be properly prepared for the events prior the Second Coming, as well as for His glorious return.

The Great Events of Human History

For many the Second Coming is often ignored and seldom talked about.

What do you think are the great events in human history? Many things may come to mind, perhaps too many to even begin to write down or give serious thought to. Possibly you thought about the creation of Adam and Eve (the beginning of the human race). Maybe you thought about the entrance of sin or the Great Flood. Most every Christian would surely mention the birth of Christ, His first coming. However, as great as these are there is still to come the greatest event of all. This time will bring the culmination all human history into one final magnificent crescendo, as it were, and it is the Second Coming.

While there appears to be great interest surrounding this season, most people continue life as normal without thought to the personal ramifications it might have. How will He come? His first coming was one of humility, grace, and mercy, but His Second Coming will be very different.

Getting the Right Perspective

So, what about this return of Christ? How should we think about it? What is the right attitude and the right approach to this coming reality? So many people ignore the Second Coming. They seldom talk about it and think about it even less. Why is the greatest event so easily crowded out for other less important thoughts and ideas? Could it be that people are apprehensive to talk about it for the following reasons?

- There is too much controversy surrounding the Lord's return.
- There are too many confusing and overwhelming ideas about the Lord's return.
- It seems impossible to sort out everything unless you are a Bible scholar.
- People say strange things, which cause others to withdraw from the discussion for fear of being associated with unusual ideas.

What should be our priorities and thinking about this momentous occasion?

Oftentimes, we want to know all the facts, the order, the sequence, and events surrounding the return of Jesus. The books of Daniel and Revelation along with other chapters in the Gospels give us a great number of details surrounding His coming. To understand this information and how it fits together is certainly a worthy endeavor. However, should this be our focus? The most important aspect of the Christ's return is the preparation of our hearts and lives. Are we ready?

Staying Focused

The future coming of Christ should act like a beacon that guides us through the treacherous waters of culture keeping us on a true course. Without this event as our focus point, we will veer onto the rocks of life. Even now, the lesser lights distract us. We have made less important events guiding beacons. Only when it is too late do we realize we were off course having lost our way.

Waiting for a Long Time

John, in the book of Revelation says Jesus is coming quickly. The challenge for us alive today is that it has been almost two-thousand years since John penned these words. How are we to remain properly focused on this extremely important event when the timing seems so exceptionally long? Jesus says on three different occasions in the last chapter of Revelation He is coming quickly. Hebrews repeats the same idea.

Revelation 22:7 "And behold, I am coming quickly. Blessed is he who heeds the words of the prophecy of this book." ((NASU))

Revelation 22:12-13 {12} "Behold, I am coming quickly, and My reward is with Me, to render to every man according to what he has done. 13 "I am the Alpha and the Omega, the first and the last, the beginning and the end." ((NASU))

Revelation 22:20 He who testifies to these things says, "Yes, I am coming quickly." Amen. Come, Lord Jesus. (NASU)

Hebrews 10:37 ...for yet in a truly little while, He who is coming will come, and will not delay. (NASU)

It is difficult to keep the nearness of Christ's coming fresh and alive when it has been such a long time coming in human terms. This tension is what we will discuss next.

The Two Big Ideas

Understanding both the nearness and the farness of the Second Coming for the Christian is a difficult task. How can Jesus' return be both near and far at the same time? It is this tension that confuses us, and we slowly drift in one direction or the other. Somehow, we need to be able to live holding both ideas in proper tension.

We need to understand how God calculates time. In 2 Peter 3:8, we see that God counts time very differently than how humans tally time.

2 Peter 3:8 But do not let this one fact escape your notice, beloved, that with the Lord one day is like a thousand years, and a thousand years like one day.

How can this be? It is because God is outside of time and sees everything in an eternal context.

Is it possible to see time as God sees it? Yes, it is possible, but it requires constant vigilance on our part. God created us in His image; so, we are able see time in His way. Unfortunately, because we choose not to view time in God's context, our perspective about time and life becomes skewed. It is a challenge to keep eternity in the forefront of our thinking.

Even though the 2nd Coming may not be mocked there is an equally destructive and dangerous attitude that some Christians have – it is carelessness and apathy.

From a human perspective two-thousand years is a considerable time. In the verses preceding 2 Peter 3:8, we see the predominant attitude people will adopt because of the long time before of His return. The ungodly will mock the Second Coming because of the long delay (humanly speaking). They have become scoffers, skeptics, and disbelievers. This is what a long delay does if the understanding and perspective is wrong.

2 Peter 3:3-9 {3} Know this first of all, that in the last days mockers will come with their mocking, following after their own lusts, 4 and saying, "Where is the promise of His coming? For ever since the fathers fell asleep,

all continues just as it was from the beginning of creation." 5 For when they maintain this, it escapes their notice that by the word of God the heavens existed long ago and the earth was formed out of water and by water, 6 through which the world at that time was destroyed, being flooded with water. 7 But by His word the present heavens and earth are being reserved for fire, kept for the day of judgment and destruction of ungodly men. 8 But do not let this one fact escape your notice, beloved, that with the Lord one day is like a thousand years, and a thousand years like one day. 9 The Lord is not slow about His promise, as some count slowness, but is patient toward you, not wishing for any to perish but for all to come to repentance. (NASU)

Mocking versus Carelessness

Christians do not mock the Second Coming, but so many live with another wrong and prevailing attitude, which is just as destructive and dangerous as mocking. It is the attitudes of carelessness and apathy. The result of both these attitudes (mocking and carelessness) lead to the same type of living – ungodly lifestyles and ungodly thinking. Jesus says fearful things to Christians who are not properly prepared for His return.

Matthew 24:45-51 {45} "Who then is the faithful and sensible slave whom his master put in charge of his household to give them their food at the proper time? 46 "Blessed is that slave whom his master finds so doing when he comes. 47 "Truly I say to you that he will put him in charge of all his possessions. 48 "But if that evil slave says in his heart, 'My master is not coming for a long time,' 49 and begins to beat his fellow slaves and eat and drink with drunkards; 50 the master of that slave will come on a day when he does not expect him and at an hour which he does not know, 51 and will cut him in pieces and assign him a place with the hypocrites; in that place there will be weeping and gnashing of teeth. (NASU)

Matthew 25:1-13 {1} "Then the kingdom of heaven will be comparable to ten virgins, who took their lamps and went out to meet the bridegroom. 2 "Five of them were foolish, and five were prudent. 3 "For when the foolish took their lamps, they took no oil with them, 4 but the prudent took oil in flasks along with their lamps. 5 "Now while the bridegroom was delaying, they all got drowsy and began to sleep. 6 "But at midnight there was a shout, 'Behold, the bridegroom! Come out to meet him.' 7 "Then all those virgins rose and trimmed their lamps. 8 "The foolish said to the prudent, 'Give us some of your oil, for our lamps are going out.' 9 "But the prudent answered, 'No, there will not be enough for us and you too; go instead to the dealers and buy some for yourselves.' 10 "And while they were going away to make the purchase, the bridegroom came, and those who were ready went in with him to the wedding feast; and the door was shut. 11 "Later the other virgins also came, saying, 'Lord, lord, open up for us.' 12 "But he answered, 'Truly I say to you, I do not know you.' 13 "Be on the alert then, for you do not know the day nor the hour. (NASU)

Luke 12:41-48 {41} Peter said, "Lord, are You addressing this parable to us, or to everyone else as well?" 42 And the Lord said, "Who then is the faithful and sensible steward, whom his master will put in charge of his servants, to give them their rations at the proper time? 43 "Blessed is that slave whom his master finds so doing when he comes. 44 "Truly I say to you that he will put him in charge of all his possessions. 45 "But if that slave says in his heart, 'My master will be a long time in coming,' and begins to beat the slaves, both men and women, and to eat and drink and get drunk; 46 the master of that slave will come on a day when he does not expect him and at an hour he does not know, and will cut him in pieces, and assign him a place with the unbelievers. 47 "And that slave who knew his master's will and did not get ready or act in accord with his will, will receive many lashes, 48 but the one who did not know it, and committed deeds worthy of a flogging, will receive but few. From everyone who has been given much, much will be required; and to whom they entrusted much, of him they will ask all the more. (NASU)

As Christians, the Day of the Lord should not come as a thief in the night. We should be fully aware of what is happening. Not being properly prepared has extremely negative eternal consequences. This is not what Jesus wants for us.

Judgement

We must remember that death is not an escape from the judgement to come.

One thought that needs attention in this introduction; it is the idea of destruction and judgement that happens at the Second Coming. Jesus' return will be glorious, but it will also be destructive. He is coming to judge the inhabitants of the earth. At this time, He will also judge the saints through rewards.

2 Peter 3:6 shows a connection with the Great Flood during Noah's lifetime and the Second Coming. Jesus draws a parallel between these two events as well in Matthew 24 and Luke 17.

Matthew 24:36-41 {36} "But of that day and hour no one knows, not even the angels of heaven, nor the Son, but the Father alone. 37 "For the coming of the Son of Man will be just like the days of Noah. 38 "For as in those days before the flood they were eating and drinking, marrying and giving in marriage, until the day that Noah entered the ark, 39 and they did not understand until the flood came and took them all away; so will the coming of the Son of Man be. 40 "Then there will be two men in the field; one will be taken, and one will be left. 41 "Two women will be grinding at the mill; one will be taken, and one will be left. (NASU)

Luke 17:26-30 {26} "And just as it happened in the days of Noah, so it will be also in the days of the Son of Man: 27 they were eating, they were drinking, they were marrying, they were being given in marriage, until the day that Noah entered the ark, and the flood came and destroyed them all. 28 "It was the same as happened in the days of Lot: they were eating, they were drinking, they were buying, they were selling, they were planting, they were building; 29 but on the day that Lot went out from Sodom it rained fire and brimstone from heaven and destroyed them all. (NASU)

We see the Great Day of the Lord is not just a casual brotherly visit by Jesus. It will be a dramatic event with dire consequences for both the unsaved and the unprepared.

Connecting the Past and the Future

Jesus dramatically connects the past judgements of Noah's flood and the fiery destruction of Sodom and Gomorrah during the time of Lot. In the day of their divine judgement the people were living life like there was no tomorrow or future judgement. They thought everything would continue as it always had in the past. However, to their own horror they were wrong.

All past generations have come and gone, but the following truths remains:

- No past generation has yet seen the Second Coming,
- Every generation and each person will stand before the Judge of the earth.
- Death is not an escape from the judgement to come.
- The believer's judgement is not about eternal damnation or punishment but is about one's faithfulness and obedience with the focus on rewards.
- God will judge severely and eternally nonbelievers for their rejection of Christ.

In the same manner as Jesus links Noah and Lot's events together, Peter also does the same. We see God has done it before, and so, we know He will do it again. All the past judgements in the Bible and historically culminate into the Final Judgement.

2 Peter 2:4-10 {4} For if God did not spare angels when they sinned, but cast them into hell and committed them to pits of darkness, reserved for judgment; 5 and did not spare the ancient world, but preserved Noah, a preacher of righteousness, with seven others, when He brought a flood upon the world of the ungodly; 6 and if He condemned the cities of Sodom and Gomorrah to destruction by reducing them to ashes, having made them

an example to those who would live ungodly lives thereafter; 7 and if He rescued righteous Lot, oppressed by the sensual conduct of unprincipled men 8 (for by what he saw and heard that righteous man, while living among them, felt his righteous soul tormented day after day by their lawless deeds), 9 then the Lord knows how to rescue the godly from temptation, and to keep the unrighteous under punishment for the day of judgment, 10 and especially those who indulge the flesh in its corrupt desires and despise authority. (NASU)

Alert and Ready

Jesus gives us ample warning, so that; we can properly prepare ourselves for His coming. At the end of the Olivet Discourse in Matthew, He tell us two things.

Matthew 24:42-44 {42} "Therefore be on the **alert**, for you do not know which day your Lord is coming. 43 "But be sure of this, that if the head of the house had known at what time of the night the thief was coming, he would have been on the alert and would not have allowed his house to be broken into. 44 "For this reason you also must be **ready**; for the Son of Man is coming at an hour when you do not think He will. (NASU)

First, in verse 42 Jesus says, "Be on the alert." This means to be vigilant, to stay awake and to watch. While we do not know the day, we can certainly know a close approximate for the time for Jesus' return.

- Alert has the idea of being aware and careful of one's personal state of being. Staying focused on eternity helps us in remaining alert.
- It is easy to become lazy and careless about one's life. Over time we lose our attentiveness. We become too comfortable and negligent.
- We must avoid the 'stupor of life'. This is when we mindlessly move through life with little thought about what we are doing and

how we are doing it. We rarely take the time for reflection and evaluation.

We cannot allow ourselves to fall asleep spiritually, for if we do, we will not be ready!

Second, in verse 44 Jesus says, "You must also be ready." This means we must be properly prepared. Now is the time to make our adjustments and prepare our hearts, minds, and emotions rather than trying to make the changes when it is too late.

- If we are awake and alert, then we can prepare ourselves. An important question to ask is this, "Am I prepared or ready for the events of the end times and the Second Coming"?
- We must have a mentality of fitness, so that we are able to endure. There is a sense of readiness about all that we are doing.

Let us use the idea of soldiering. What does it take to be a good soldier?

Alert – a soldier must always remain on high alert, paying close attention to all that is happening around him. He can never become lazy, careless, or sleepy when he is fighting in a war. A vigilant soldier is a soldier who stays alive.

Ready – a soldier must always be mentally and physically prepared for the difficulty of fighting in a war. This readiness begins in boot camp and continues for as long as he is a soldier. He is always preparing. He must remain in top physical condition, and he keeps all his weapons and equipment in that same condition. At a moment's notice, when his leader commands, he moves even into harm's way.

Parables of Preparation

At the end of the Mt. Olivet discourse in Matthew, Jesus gives four parables that speak about alertness and readiness. Jesus is setting the challenge before us. What will we choose?

In the first three parables, we are able to see a common four-part theme.

- A master and followers
- A long delay
- A time of testing
- An unexpected return

A quick summary of the first three parables describes three aspects of preparation. (1) Jesus tells us to prepare. (2) He leaves us the choice as to how we prepare. (3) He requires that we live with the result of our preparations.

1. Right versus Wrong Preparation (Matthew 24:45-51) – this is the story of the slave / master. The slave does the wrong things because the master delays.

The focus of this parable is a willful choosing to disobey. This person shows intentional carelessness and disinterest in what Jesus requires. We must obey all that Jesus commands.

Matthew 24:45-51 {45} "Who then is the faithful and sensible slave whom his master put in charge of his household to give them their food at the proper time? 46 "Blessed is that slave whom his master finds so doing when he comes. 47 "Truly I say to you that he will put him in charge of all his possessions. 48 "But if that evil slave says in his heart, 'My master is not coming for a long time,' 49 and begins to beat his fellow slaves and eat and drink with drunkards; 50 the master of that slave will come on a day when he does not expect him and at an hour which he does not know, 51 and will cut him in pieces and assign him a place with the hypocrites; in that place there will be weeping and gnashing of teeth. (NASU)

2. Complete versus Partial Preparation (Matthew 25:1-13) – this is the story of the ten virgins. Five virgins are properly and completely prepared and five were foolish in that they were only partially prepared due to the long delay.

(Note: while verse two says they took no oil with them, we see that their lamps were burning in verse eight. What Jesus is saying in verse two is that the foolish virgins did not take any **extra** oil with them, they ran out).

The focus of this parable is dealing with personal sin. Personal sins that we choose not quit quenches the work of the Holy Spirit. This neglect leaves us unprepared and apathetic. Sin makes it so we cannot properly prepare for difficult times. Suddenly, then it is too late.

Matthew 25:1-13 {1} "Then the kingdom of heaven will be comparable to ten virgins, who took their lamps and went out to meet the bridegroom. 2 "Five of them were foolish, and five were prudent. 3 "For when the foolish took their lamps, they took no oil with them, 4 but the prudent took oil in flasks along with their lamps. 5 "Now while the bridegroom was delaying, they all got drowsy and began to sleep. 6 "But at midnight there was a shout, 'Behold, the bridegroom! Come out to meet him.' 7 "Then all those virgins rose and trimmed their lamps. 8 "The foolish said to the prudent, 'Give us some of your oil, for our lamps are going out.' 9 "But the prudent answered, 'No, there will not be enough for us and you too; go instead to the dealers and buy some for yourselves.' 10 "And while they were going away to make the purchase, the bridegroom came, and those who were ready went in with him to the wedding feast; and the door was shut. 11 "Later the other virgins also came, saying, 'Lord, lord, open up for us.' 12 "But he answered, 'Truly I say to you, I do not know you.' 13 "Be on the alert then, for you do not know the day nor the hour. (NASU)

3. Willing versus Unwilling Preparation (Matthew 25:14-30) - this is the three steward's story. Two stewards were willing to prepare and one was not willing to prepare during the long delay.

The focus of this parable is faithfulness and obedience. To be alert and ready we must be willing to be faithful and obedient. It is always better to be diligent rather than lazy. Laziness may seem easier throughout a responsibility, but the price paid at the end for being lazy will always be far greater than all the work that we should have done.

Matthew 25:14-31 {14} "For it is just like a man about to go on a journey, who called his own slaves and entrusted his possessions to them. 15 "To one he gave five talents, to another, two, and to another, one, each according to his own ability; and he went on his journey. 16 "Immediately the one who had received the five talents went and traded with them, and gained five more talents. 17 "In the same manner the one who had received the two talents gained two more. 18 "But he who received the one talent went away, and dug a hole in the ground and hid his master's money. 19 "Now after a long time the master of those slaves came and settled accounts with them. 20 "The one who had received the five talents came up and brought five more talents, saying, 'Master, you entrusted five talents to me. See, I have gained five more talents.' 21 "His master said to him, 'Well done, good and faithful slave. You were faithful with a few things, I will put you in charge of many things; enter into the joy of your master.' 22 "Also the one who had received the two talents came up and said, 'Master, you entrusted two talents to me. See, I have gained two more talents.' 23 "His master said to him, 'Well done, good and faithful slave. You were faithful with a few things, I will put you in charge of many things; enter into the joy of your master.' 24 "And the one also who had received the one talent came up and said, 'Master, I knew you to be a hard man, reaping where you did not sow and gathering where you scattered no seed. 25 'And I was afraid, and went away and hid your talent in the ground. See, you have what is yours.' 26 "But his master answered and said to him, 'You wicked, lazy slave, you knew that I reap where I did not sow and gather where I scattered no seed. 27 'Then you ought to have put my money in the bank, and on my arrival I would have received my money back with interest. 28 'Therefore take away the talent from him, and give it to the one who has the ten talents.' 29 "For to everyone who has, more shall be given, and he will have an abundance;

but from the one who does not have, even what he does have shall be taken away. 30 "Throw out the worthless slave into the outer darkness; in that place there will be weeping and gnashing of teeth. (NASU)

These three parables tell us the importance of obedience, faithfulness and diligently dealing with personal sin. If we do these things, then we will be properly prepared and will receive our reward.

The fourth parable is different from the first three. In this parable we see the results of good and poor preparation. The consequences are severe for poor preparation.

4. Fruits / Rewards of Preparation (Matthew 25:31-46) - this is the story of the sheep and goats. Those who have prepared rightly, completely, and willingly are rewarded by Jesus. He punishes those who have prepared wrongly, partially, and unwillingly. We decide, reward or punishment.

Matthew 25:31-46 {31} "But when the Son of Man comes in His glory, and all the angels with Him, then He will sit on His glorious throne. 32 "All the nations will be gathered before Him; and He will separate them from one another, as the shepherd separates the sheep from the goats; 33 and He will put the sheep on His right, and the goats on the left. 34 "Then the King will say to those on His right, 'Come, you who are blessed of My Father, inherit the kingdom prepared for you from the foundation of the world. 35 'For I was hungry, and you gave Me something to eat; I was thirsty, and you gave Me something to drink; I was a stranger, and you invited Me in; 36 naked, and you clothed Me; I was sick, and you visited Me; I was in prison, and you came to Me.' 37 "Then the righteous will answer Him, 'Lord, when did we see You hungry, and feed You, or thirsty, and give You something to drink? 38 'And when did we see You a stranger, and invite You in, or naked, and clothe You? 39 'When did we see You sick, or in prison, and come to You?' 40 "The King will answer and say to them, 'Truly I say to you, to the extent that you did it to one of these brothers of Mine, even the least of them, you did it to Me.' 41 "Then He will also say to those on His left, 'Depart from Me, accursed ones, into the eternal fire which has been prepared for the devil and his angels; 42 for I was hungry, and you gave Me nothing to eat; I was thirsty, and you gave Me nothing to drink; 43 I was a stranger, and you did not invite Me in; naked, and you did not clothe Me; sick, and in prison, and you did not visit Me.' 44 "Then they themselves also will answer, 'Lord, when did we see You hungry, or thirsty, or a stranger, or naked, or sick, or in prison, and did not take care of You?' 45 "Then He will answer them, 'Truly I say to you, to the extent that you did not do it to one of the least of these, you did not do it to Me.' 46 "These will go away into eternal punishment, but the righteous into eternal life." (NASU)

We are always to remain alert and ready for the Second Coming of Jesus. If we slack, are careless, or become apathetic we will suffer greatly.

There is a point to consider about our physical death. Death and the Second Coming are the same, in that, our time ends. We can no longer do what we should have done, nor undo what we should not have done. Whether or not we see the physical return of Jesus or we die, we must live our lives as if He were returning today. There is no second chance.

Lessons to Learn

What are Jesus and Peter trying to tell us? What are the lessons that they want us to learn and know?

1. There are three groups. What group do you think you are in?

- Group 1: scoffers of the Second Coming (usually nonbelievers).
- Group 2: careless and apathetic about the Second Coming. (unprepared believers)
- Both these groups live in a manner that does not consider eternity. Group two is intellectually interested in the Second Coming, but their lifestyles or choices are little affected.
- Group 3: alert and ready for the Second Coming (prepared believers)

2. Due to the wickedness of humanity, God destroyed the world with a flood, and He destroyed Sodom and Gomorrah with fire. (Genesis 6:11-13; 18:20-19:24).

- We know just as these two judgements happened, so will it be at the Second Coming of Christ.

3. The heart and mind of the believer must prepare for the Second Coming.

- The attitude that Jesus will be a long time in coming (even if this is true in a human context) becomes problematic.
- No matter when Jesus comes, it will be the same for everyone. We all will give an account of our life to Christ.

Revelation 22:12-13 Jesus tells us when He comes, He is bringing His reward with Him, and He will give to each of us what is due.

- We dare not live for ourselves or live as if this life on earth is all there is.
- There is a future eternity. To live in a short-sighted manner leads to undesirable consequences.
- There is no way in which to increase or decrease our rewards after death. They are set for eternity.

How we live, think, believe, and act on this earth matters. We can choose to live for ourselves, our comfort, and our own desires; or we can live life for Christ and Him alone. We must contemplate our values and priorities, and our goals and purposes.

Questions to Ponder

1. How did the idea of reaching all the UUPGs by 2022 affect your current thinking?
2. What things are hindering me from thinking deeply about the Second Coming? What do I need to do about these hinderances?
3. What pressures make it difficult to keep the Second Coming as a high priority in my life?
4. What values or priorities does my current lifestyle convey? Is my focus this life or eternity?
5. What emotion(s) do I feel when I think about the Second Coming? Why?
6. In what ways am I using my life to bring God honor and glory, so He can say, "Well done good and faithful servant"?

TWO

ALERT AND READY: THROUGH THE REVELATION JESUS

A revelation of Jesus Christ in His glory generates alertness and readiness

Revelation as a Template

The primary purpose of Revelation was not meant to be a teaching on eschology. Jesus was not sending letters to the seven churches to satisfy their curiosity about the future. They were struggling with the difficulties in the present. These churches were suffering great persecution and they needed to be encouraged and built up. The whole book of Revelation is showing us that no matter what happens and how difficult it becomes, God is still in control.

The first three chapters in Revelation will be our guide on how to be alert and properly prepared for the Second Coming. Jesus is speaking to the leaders and people of the seven churches in Asia. Jesus knows what being alert and prepared looks like and how to do it.

Even though these letters are directed to churches in Asia, they are equally applicable for us today. In one sense, very little has changed in how people relate to their environment in two-thousand years. We struggle with the same troubles and difficulties as they did. For example, they had money problems, relationship problems, wrong values, wrong priorities, and struggled with sin. We are still dealing with the same distractions today.

The things Jesus emphasizes in His letters will surprise us as He mentions things that most people would not think about. Jesus knows what is important so He focuses on the key preparation factors every Christian should consider. As we begin to read chapters two and three, we will see that Jesus repeats Himself. It is not just because the different churches have the same problem. He repeats Himself to emphasize the things He considers most important. As we move through these two chapters we also will repeat, following Jesus' pattern and emphasizing the things He emphasized.

The first message of Revelation is the preparation of heart and mind. Jesus Himself does not talk primarily about the details, the timing, and events that will unfold before His coming. Instead, He emphasizes the preparation of heart and the mind. Revelation does give hundreds of details concerning the events in the Last Days, but the first three chapters where Jesus speaks directly is focused on one message: Be alert and ready.

Our primary focus needs to be preparing our hearts and minds. We should try to discern the times and the details surrounding His Second Coming, but this is not the first thing. Throughout the Bible there are plenty of details about these events and their timing. They are exciting to study, but if we are not in the right place spiritually, it will be a disaster for us.

Perspective of Jesus

John says in the first three verses, "These are things that must soon take place" and "also the time is near." What Jesus said to the seven churches happened, but much of Revelation has not. It has been nearly 2,000 years since John wrote these words, "the time is near". So, again we are reminded how God calculates time is quite different from us. We must work to cultivate God's perspective.

Revelation 1:1-3 {1}The Revelation of Jesus Christ, which God gave Him to show to His bond-servants, the things which must soon take place; and He sent and communicated it by His angel to His bond-servant John, 2 who testified to the word of God and to the testimony of Jesus Christ, even to all that he saw. 3 Blessed is he who reads and those who hear the words of the prophecy, and heed the things which are written in it; for the time is near.

It is imperative to develop the mindset that Jesus is coming soon. This can only be done if we have an eternal perspective. We must be careful that we do not get caught up with living our life here only on earth. When this happens the things in this life gain too much importance. This life is the temporal and it will pass away.

The Mindset of John

John is setting the tone for the book in verse nine. The reason John is on the island of Patmos is due to his Christian witness. He is suffering persecution for following Christ.

Revelation 1:9 I, John, your brother and fellow partaker in the tribulation and kingdom and perseverance which are in Jesus, was on the island called Patmos because of the word of God and the testimony of Jesus. (NASU)

We are going to focus on three words in particular.

- Tribulation – The churches were suffering severe persecution at this time. This was considered the normal Christian life.
- Kingdom – The reason for the suffering was because of the kingdom of God. The Romans Empire was threatened by this new kingdom, and did not view this idea favorably.
- Perseverance – to be faithful in God's kingdom we must patiently endure our tribulation and suffering.

As present-day believers we must have the same type of thinking as John. Without this mindset we will flounder and be unable to endure suffering properly.

A Revelation of the Glory of Jesus

Chapter one starts with a revelation of the ascended Lord Jesus Christ in all of His glory and majesty. This book ends in the same manner describing the majesty of God. For us to understand the book of Revelation and how to be prepared we first need to have a revelation of Jesus.

Before John shares his vision of the risen Christ, he narrates specific characteristics of Jesus that frame in what is needed to be alert and prepared.

We stand in the revelation of God's grace and because of His grace we have peace with Him. Understanding God's grace correctly is critical in our preparation. Grace is not an excuse to sin, but the power to overcome sin. Peace is a stability factor in the midst of unstable times. We need to be on the right side of God and remain there. This is done by faith through grace.

We must have a revelation of God's sovereignty. God is transcendent (in and outside His creation). He is sovereign over all. Creation cannot move or delay His will. God is in the present, as He was the past. Even more importantly we must remember He is in the future. However he is not just in the future, but He controls the future.

John's introduces the Godhead; we see God the Father, God the Holy Spirit, and God the Son. The Trinity works together in creation moving things along to the end of the age. This is God's doing and not man's.

Jesus is the Faithful Witness. What He knows and sees, He tells us so we can remain alert and ready. What He says is true and this is to remind us that He knows all things.

He is the firstborn from the dead, meaning we no longer need to fear death or the things that may cause that death. We have the assurance of eternal life.

Reading Revelation can be a scary thing, but John informs us that Jesus is the ruler of the kings of the earth. While it may seem that evil and wicked leaders are running rampant, they are not. God who is gracious and merciful gives the wicked opportunity and time to repent. Everything and everyone is always answerable and under the authority of the King of kings.

We need a fresh revelation of Jesus' forgiveness to save us from our sins. Our sins are the true enemy of our souls; and if His blood does not release us from the eternal consequences of sin, then what we read happening in Revelation is only minor compared to an eternity in hell. The forgiveness of our sins helps us maintain the right perspective.

We have much to look forward to after the terror of the end times. We will reign with Jesus for eternity. We must look past the darkness of the day to that glorious day. This hope will sustain us.

Never again will evil and wickeness contaminate us. We will forever enjoy the glory and dominion of God. This is our great hope and we must never lose sight of it.

We are comforted that all sorrow, pain, and suffering will end when He returns with the clouds. All will see Him, even those who have rejected Him. For them it will be a day of great mourning, but for us who are in Christ it will be a wonderful day, because it will be a time of rewards and joy.

John ends his introduction with the revelation of Christ with us. This time it is Jesus speaking. "I am the Alpha and Omega, who is and who was and who is to come." Jesus is always present with us – He will never leave us or forsake us. Nothing will happen outside of what God has already prede-cided. What a great comfort for us in the midst of the greate turmoil and distress of these times.

Revelation Through Prayer

John was praying when he hears the trumpet sounding voice of glorious Jesus. If we are going to have any meaningful revelation of Jesus, we need to be ferevently praying. Startled, he turns to see who is speaking. The last time John heard the Lord's voice was sixty years ago when Jesus was taken up to heaven. However, John was not prepared for what he saw.

Remember that John was the closest of all the disciples to Jesus. He walked intimately with Jesus for three and one-half years. Yet, when He sees Jesus in His glory and majesty, he is overwhelmed with fear and falls down as a dead man. Jesus in His glory is both terrifying and wonderful at the same time.

Surviving the events of the last days in a God-honoring fashion requires we see Jesus differently, more gloriously. The gospels showed His humanness; but Revelation show us His glory and majesty, and this is exactly what John saw and it is what we shows His glory. It is this revelation of Jesus that will carry us through to the end. The turmoil of the end times will require each of us to have a revelation of the glory and power of Jesus

Revelation Through Scripture

We may never have a vision or divine relelation as John did. However, we can see Him through the scriptures in this manner by meditating on the attributes and glory of Jesus. This is best done before the difficult times come. Learning how to swim while you are drowning is a bad idea. We must prepare beforehand.

Revelation Through God Revealing Himself in Suffering

Job also had a divine revelation of God in the midst of the most difficult time of his life. In one day Job literally lost everything he owned, and his children died as well. He is tormented by Satan in his physical body wishing he could die. He regreted the day he had been born. Several times he asked God, "Why?" but there was only silence. God eventually reveals Himself in a whirlwind speaking to Job. However, God never answers any of Job's questions or brings understanding to his suffering. Job just having a revelation of God in the whirlwind was sufficient for him.

Getting Started

Jesus methodically tells us what to do to be alert and ready in chapters two and three. We see the great love and concern He has for His church. He explains what it means and what it takes to be ready for His return. The information He gives us is invaluable.

In the letters Jesus is either going to commend, warn, or rebuke them. He gives every church a promise if they remain alert and ready for His coming by being faithful and persevering.

As we work through each letter Jesus shows us how to prepare, what to think, what attitudes to have, what to do, and what not to do. He warns us to take care of our spiritual life and to overcome...never giving up! Eight times the word 'repent' is used in chapters two and three. We must approach these last days with a spirit of humility always checking our hearts. We must continually ask the question, "Where do I need to change my thinking to align with God's thinking? This is the core of repentance.

In the next few chapters of Revelation, Jesus gives us examples of seven churches who were at different stages of alertness and readiness. From them we can learn vital principles we need to incorporate into our lives.

THREE

ALERT AND READY: LESSONS FROM EPHESUS

(REVELATION 2:1-7)

The church of Ephesus was doing everything right, but they still left their first love because of personal sin.

Ephesus was one of the three most influential cities in the eastern part of the Roman Empire. Paul ministered in this city for three years warning the believers that false teachers would come and draw people away from the faith (see Acts 20:29–31). Indeed, false teachers did cause problems in the Ephesian church, but they resisted them. We see this through Paul's letters to Timothy. He stayed in Ephesus after Paul left for Macedonia. John also ministered in this city and knew that these believers had resisted false teaching (2:2).[1]

1. Jesus says, "The One who holds the seven stars in His right hand, the One who walks among the seven golden lampstands, says this:" (NASU)

The Ephesians know that Jesus is in control of His church. He walks through His church observing everything and everyone.

As Christians today, we would do well to understand that omniscience, omnipresence and all-powerful Jesus. Immediately, we see the inference to the fear of the Lord. This is one of the greatest awarenesses we can have in preparing for the Last Days.

2. Jesus says, "I know your deeds and your toil and perseverance," (NASU)

The Ephesians did not grow weary in their deeds, work or perseverance. The word 'work' as used here has the idea of 'toiling to the point of exhaustion'.

We are not to become spiritually lazy and careless. We must work hard, persevere, endure, never giving up. We must always please and honor God in all we do. Even when things are difficult and we have served God for years, we cannot become careless thinking that we can coast to the end.

3. Jesus says, "You cannot tolerate evil men," (NASU)

The Ephesians refused to tolerate evil men. They did not try to be politically correct when dealing with evil men. These men would destroy the church, as they were wolves in sheep's clothing. Interestingly, the word tolerate comes from a base word 'foot'. These men were given the boot of the left foot. They were removed from the congregation.

We need to be able to identify evil men. Who are these evil men? These would be men who speak contrary to what the Bible says. We are not to allow them a place in the church. The church is meant to be a place of safety and security. The present day church must be very discerning as to who they listen to. There are many evil men who are only seeking their own glory and agenda.

4. Jesus says, "You put to the test those who call themselves apostles, and they are not, and you found them to be false." (NASU)

The Ephesians tested apostles, (they scrutinized and examined them). There were not only evil men who wanted to destroy the church, but there were false apostles, prophets and teacher. They sought to put them to the test to determine in they were genuine.

We must test spiritual authorities to see if they are true and genunine. Nowhere in the scriptures are we told just to accept leaders. Leaders need to be tested to see if they are true. What is their character? (I purposely did not use the word sincere, as there are many leaders who are sincere, but they are not true to the Word of God.) It is not gifting, charisma, or personality we should be considering, but character. A false leader cannot produce good fruit (character), because his roots are evil.

5. Jesus says, "You have perseverance and have endured for My name's sake, and have not grown weary." (NASU)

The Ephesian church was hard working and were tireless never becoming weary in their well doing. They also knew how to endure suffering and do it well. This was a great church and they were well commended.

Jesus sees what we are doing and commend us. One of the big themes in these letters is the ability to suffer with patience and perseverance. It would do each of us well to think deeply about our ablity to suffer. What happens to us when trouble or difficulty comes our way? Do we veer into fear, worry, frustration, anxiety, anger, or resentment? Are we able to genuinely rejoice and give thanks? If we have answered the last negatively, then we need to reconsider our thinking and choices.

6. Jesus says, "But I have this against you, that you have left your first love." (NASU)

The Ephesians were rebuked for leaving their first love. How could they be doing so good and have something this wrong? They were not guarding their hearts. The church would not tolerate evil in others, but they were tolerating evil in their personal lives.

Notice it does not say you have lost your first love, but you have left your first love. There is a careless intentionality about this leaving. The relationship with Jesus grew cold and indifferent. We must maintain fervor, passion and zeal for Jesus. This relationship must remain fresh and alive.

What is it that causes a relationship with Jesus to grow cold, so we leave our first love?

Matthew 24:12 "...lawlessness is increased, most people's love will grow cold. (NASU)

Sin causes our love to grow cold and stale. For this reason they were called to repent. We are to stop sinning and do what we did when we first came to Jesus. We were sold out to Jesus and we would not tolerate sin in our lives. All sins destroy our love and fervency for the Lord. Slowly our love for Jesus ebbs away and our hearts grow cold because of sin.

In verse five the word 'repent' is used twice. Unfortuanately, this is one of the many words the church today has dropped and eliminated, because the word has been deemed 'too offensive' or 'too strong' and people will get their feelings hurt. However, Jesus used this word as He spoke to His church; so obviously, He was more concerned about their soul than about their feelings.

The word repent simply means 'to change your thinking'. However, we can easily change one wrong way of thinking with another. In order to avoid this catastrophe, we need to narrow down the idea. Repentance then is 'I agree to think what God says'. Repentance does not allow us to create reasons or make excuses as to why we think incorrectly or why we behave sinfully. God narrows down our thinking to align with His thinking, so that we find ourselves responding to things as He would respond.

If our thinking changes, it will change both what we believe and what we do. If we are still tolerating sin in our lives, then we have not repented (changed our thinking to agree with what God says). We must daily live a lifestyle of continual repentance.

This warning is severe. Jesus says, "I am coming and when I come I will remove your lampstand out of its place unless you repent" (NASU) Jesus does not tolerate sin in our lives. He expects us to repent, to stop sinning.

7. Jesus says, "Yet this you do have, that you hate the deeds of the Nicolaitans, which I also hate." (NASU)

The Ephesians hated the deeds of the Nicolaitans, which Jesus also hated. In the days of the early church there were many false doctrines and teaching. It is obvious that the Epheisan church really understood their Bible and listened carefully to true apostles. This church would not tolerate evil men, tested apostles for genuiness, and hated the deeds of the Nicolaitans.

Who were the Nicolaitans and what did they do? It is not clear who they were, but it is thought they were a cult (perhaps started by Nicholas one of the seven who waited tables in Acts 4). This group it seems used their freedom given by grace for sinful pleasures and careless liberties. They taught it is was perfectly okay to eat foods offered to idols and sexual immorality was acceptable. This practice showed a lack of concern for others, especially the weaker brothers.

Note: The Nicoliatans could be likened to those who were the liberals and modernists of the day. These people (the Niocolaitans) of the time, felt that the church was too strict and rigid. It was out of step with the times and the culture...the church was no longer relatable. The Nicolaitans believed that the church needed to lighten up its stance on right and wrong, and morality. And so it is today, in that, many say the church is no longer relatable to the culture. However, the truth be told, the church should never compromise in order to be relatable or relative to the culture.

8. The Ephesian promise: overcomers can eat from the tree of life. An overcomer is one who is victorious and persevering in the face of conflict and hardship.

It is important to remember that sinful Adam and Eve were banned from eating from this tree of life. We must persevere to overcome sin. Choosing to tolerate sin in our lives could mean we will lose the right to eat of this tree for the second time.

Proverbs 11:30 tells us that the fruit of righteous is a tree of life. When we practice righteousness we are eating from the tree of life. Choosing to practice and tolerate sin becomes a tree of death.

The Ephesians did a lot of good and right things, but the sin in their personal lives is what caused their love for Jesus to grow cold.

Matthew 7:21-23 {21} "Not everyone who says to Me, 'Lord, Lord,' will enter the kingdom of heaven, but he who does the will of My Father who is in heaven will enter. 22 "Many will say to Me on that day, 'Lord, Lord, did we not prophesy in Your name, and in Your name cast out demons, and in Your name perform many miracles?' 23 "And then I will declare to them, 'I never knew you; DEPART FROM ME, YOU WHO PRACTICE LAWLESSNESS.' (NASU)

These verses describe those who did not overcome sin. We must be determined to overcome sin.

Questions to Ponder from Ephesus

1. What is our heart attitude towards difficult situations in our lives? Are we persevering through difficulty or have we given up due to weariness?
2. Are we tolerating evil people through our friendships?
3. Do we review all that is being told us by comparing it to what the Bible says?
4. Do we accept an authority figure before we test his claims?
5. Are we passionate about Jesus, about obeying Him, about bringing honor and glory to Him?
6. Do we tolerate sinful desires in our hearts? Have we grown comfortable with compromise? Do we justify ourselves even if we are living contrary to God's ways?

FOUR

ALERT AND READY: LESSONS FROM SMYRNA

Revelation 2:8-11: The church of Smyrna suffered greatly but they never quit being faithful to Jesus. They never lost their eternal perspective. Jesus neither warned nor rebuked this church.

Smyrna was a center for the cult of emperor worship. During the reign of emperor Domitian (who ruled from A.D. 81 to 96), the government demanded emperor worship for all Roman citizens. Those who refused could receive the death penalty. Once a year, all citizens burned incense on an altar to Caesar. Once done, they would receive a certificate proving that they had done their civil duty. While this was more an act of political loyalty than a religious act, the citizen had to say, while burning the incense, "Caesar is lord." Many Christians considered this act blasphemous and refused to do it.

Smyrna had a large Jewish population that actively opposed the Christians. So, the church in this city struggled against two hostile forces. First, the

Gentile population loyal to Rome supported emperor worship, and secondly, the large Jewish population that strongly opposed Christianity. Persecution and suffering were inevitable in this kind of environment.

Christ encouraged this small church that both the Gentiles and the Jew persecuted. The persecution nearly snuffed the church out. Jesus said, "I am the First and the Last, who died and is alive" (see 1:17–18). Even though the church was almost dead because of persecution, Christ was reminding them that he was sovereign and eternal. Even if believers suffered to the point of death, Christ, the one who "came to life again," would raise them to eternal life with him.[1]

This perspective and understanding would have been a great encouragement to the church as they suffered greatly through persecution. There are only two churches out of the seven that Jesus commends without any warning or rebuke. This is one of those two churches.

The church in Smyrna would have had to carefully weigh the cost of compromise. They chose well, but their choice caused severe persecution. We should pause and reflect on our willingness to suffer for Christ.

1. Jesus says, "The first and the last, who was dead, and has come to life, says this:" (NASU)

This statement would give the church the eternal perspective that they so desperately needed. Nothing can happen outside of Jesus as He is the beginning and the end, the first and the last. Even death in its earthly finality is nothing to a resurrected Lord.

Without an eternal perspective nothing in the realm of suffering makes any sense. Suffering clouds our understanding about life and about God. We must continually remind ourselves of God's eternity and our eternity. It does not make difficulty easy, but it does make difficulty bearable (with the right attitudes).

2. Jesus says, "I know your tribulation." (NASU)

Jesus telling the Christians in Smyrna that He knew they were suffering was a great comfort. They would wonder if God had forgotten them, as this is normal human thinking. However, Jesus wanted them to know that He did not forget about them. He was aware and watching all that was happeing to them. The grace of Jesus would be sufficient for them in the midst of their persecution.

There is a empathy that Jesus shows us. He is able to give us this empathy because He also suffered to the point of death. This is not some mechanical exercise because it is the right thing to say. It is deeply heartfelt and genuine.

Jesus knows and is aware of our tribulations. This tribulation is suffering that comes to us from others, because we have choosen to live a righteous life. We should not confuse this godly suffering with trouble we have created as a result of our sinful choices and poor decisions. Peter says if we do wrong and suffer for it there is no glory in this suffering; but if we suffer for the sake of Christ we are blessed and happy.

We must be willing to suffer for Christ. We cannot make compromises in our daily walk of faith to avoid suffering and persecution. Avoidance of suffering is easy for us to do and even think it is okay. We willingly believe lies in order to convince ourselves we are not denying Christ. However, if we compromise on what we consider small "unimportant" issues to avoid suffering, then what will we do when the cost to us is personally high?

3. Jesus says, "I know your poverty (but you are rich)." (NASU)

The tribulation of these believers caused their poverty. This would certainly include economic hardship, but also a lack of influence, no control, lack of opportunity, lack of safety and security. The list could go on. Even though they are poor in every natural aspect, Jesus says they are rich (spiritually). These believers kept the right perspective and understanding in the midst of tremendous trouble.

Jesus is willing to again suffer with us, even though He has already suffered.

Often we think we are willing to suffer for Jesus until we begin to suffer. When this happens, we think this is not what we want or agreed to, but it is. Jesus promises us suffering and persecution if we are going to follow Him. We need to approach these last days with a correct mindset. The goal is not trying to decrease our suffering and difficulties, but learn how to thrive in them. We are often looking for a way to escape, and unfortunately our way of escape often requires us to compromise.

Paul in 1 Corinthians 10:13 tells us that our way of escape is to be able to endure our suffering or temptation. It is quite human to look for a way out of suffering, but this is not a godly idea. Psalms 23 says that even though we walk in the valley of the shadow of death, we will fear no evil for you are with us. Jesus is willing to again suffer with us, even though He has already suffered. We never suffer alone.

4. Jesus says, "I know the blasphemy by those who say they are Jews and are not, but are a synagogue of Satan." (NASU)

These believers were suffering ridicule, betrayal, and blasphemy from the false religious community. The Christians were following God correctly, and they were being persecuted by those who were not. It was the Jewish community that was betraying the Christians by being informers agaisnt them on behalf of the government.

If we are following God with all our hearts, then other "pseudo religious" poeple will become antagonistic toward us. They will ridicule and shame those who are truly committed to Christ. In the last days we can expect persecution to come from governmental authorities, as well as the false religious community. We should not be shocked by this. We may well be surprised at who is marginalizing and persecuting us.

It is unfortunate but true that much of the persecution that genuine Christians have endured came from religious people. Some even make the claim that they are followers of Jesus. This can be quite disconcerting and confusing. It has happened historically and it will happen again. Whenever we speak the truth, those who do not love the truth (practice it) will not only reject the truth, but also marginalize and even persecute the truth sayers.

5. Jesus says, "Do not fear what you are about to suffer." (NASU)

They were commanded not to fear what they were going to suffer and suffer greatly they did. They were thrown into prison and would be killed. It was not an easy life for them, but nonetheless they were told not fear.

How is this even possible? How can we not fear suffering and death?

This is a difficult command as suffering is not enjoyable but painful on many levels. In order not to fear we must have a strong eternal perspective and trust in God. We must consider suffering for Christ a privilege. Allowing fear into our hearts will create a lack of faith, peace, and joy. Rather than overcoming suffering the suffering will overcome us.

If we fear God sufficiently, we will fear nothing else.

God is not expecting us to enjoy persecution and suffering, but He is demanding that we not fear them. God's grace will be sufficient for us during these times.

Fear, worry and anxiety are sin. We are commanded not to fear. Besides being a sin, fear and worry are things that take root and grow in our lives. Fear is insatiable, always demanding more compromise. When we fear we complain and lose heart. It is only our absolute trust in the Lord that will sustain us.

It is impossible to trust God and fear at the same time. Our fear and worry betray our lack of trust in God. Not only is fear and worry a sin, but our lack of trust in God is also a sin. We are choosing to believe lies that God is not good, or God does not love me, or God is not able to protect me.

There are levels or degrees of persecution. If we are embarrassed about our Christianity now, how will we do if we receive...?

- Ridicule – mocking, scoffing, name calling, threats, and insults
- Loss of – opportunities, material possessions, status, relationships, freedom, and honor
- Bodily harm – torture, physical pain, death

Are we willing to suffer persecution in the manner of ridicule, loss, or bodily harm? We are not to fear him who can destroy the body but fear Him who can destroy both body and soul in hell, (Matthew 10:28). If we fear God sufficiently, then we will fear nothing else.

6. Jesus says, "Behold, the devil is about to cast some of you into prison, so that you will be tested, and you will have tribulation for ten days." (NASU)

Jesus is giving Christians of Smyrna some very difficult news. He is prophesying difficulty. The devil is going to throw some believers of Symrna into prison for the purpose of being tested. The idea of ten days suggests a short time rather than ten literal days. (However, remember God does not calculate time as we do.)

Our thinking and believing of who God is must align with Bible, rather than our own ill-conceived ideas.

This is a troublesome concept. Yes, not only does God knows what will happen, but He also allows it to happen. God does allow Satan, who is the devil, to harass us and cause us difficulty. The idea of this will upset many, but this is because pastors and teachers in the churches today have said things that are not completely true and in some cases completely false. The result of this wrong teaching is that people are not prepared for suffering currently or the immense suffering that is to come. The true reality is that our source of suffering is immaterial, (except self-inflicted suffering due to sinful choices.)

The story of Job is one example of many found in the scriptures about God and suffering. God actually gave Satan permission to harass Job. Satan was allowed by God to take away all of Job's worldly possessions and even kill his children. In addtion, Satan was given the permission to make Job sick. God has very different ideas about what He does and allows; quite different from what many Christians think. Our thinking and believing of who God is must align with the Bible, rather than our own ill-conceived ideas. We must not create a false God!

Covid-19 is unfortunately a another sad example of fear. Many Christians are fearful and afraid, so much so, it has dramatically altered their lifestyle. They will not go places or do things even though they can, because of fear. How can we truly love and minister to others if we are deathly afraid. When a plague spread through their city, most people fled for safety in the countryside, away from the sick and dying. But the early church believers intentionally put themselves in harms way by remaining in the plague-ridden city to care for the dying and sick. They loved and served these people to the point of their own death. It was this example of sacrificial love that ignited the growth of the early church. This Covid-19 virus is meant to be a wakeup call to all believers and is a small test compared to what is to come.

Are we truly prepared to die for Christ? If we cannot handle the pressures to compromise, or the ridicule, or rejection from the world now, then it is highly questionable that we are ready to die for Christ. We need to honestly and seriously think about how we are managing negative pressure from everything and everyone around us. Are we responding correctly, i.e., are we willing to suffer loss now?

7. Jesus says, "Be faithful until death, and I will give you the crown of life." (NASU)

Jesus is extending hope to the Christians of Smyrna. Their suffering is not in vain. It is greatly rewarded. Even though it will be extremely difficult for them, Jesus is encouraging them to remain faithful...do not give up. He wants the believers to think about eternity and the reward they will receive. It is a crown of life.

God is looking for faithfulness, not excuses. We have so many reasons why we choose not to suffer. Many are looking for the easy way, but Jesus told us that narrow is the gate and the way, and only a few find it. Let each of us be one of the few.

The eternal crown of life is far superior to any temporal gain we may get in this life. This is easy to say, but it is difficult to live in real life. The pull of this world is strong. We must strive for the eternal crown of life rather than striving to get ahead in this life or to even save ourlives. Our goal cannot be to have the easy life, or making money to buy stuff we cannot take with us into eternity.

8. The Smyrna Promise: He who overcomes, the one who is victorious and perseveres in the face of conflict and hardship) will not be hurt in the second death.

God's promise to the Smyrna Christians was not an easy life now, but a life with Him for eternity. They did not need to fear the second death. They would be safe forever and ever.

For us death is not the end, but only a shift. We need to take care that we do not view death as an end. It is not! We will continue on with an ever-lasting life with God. Death is however, something we must seriously consider, as it helps put things into perspective. We need to realize there is more to life than this life. It is better to suffer in this life, than to suffer forever for eternity in hell. The implication should we fail in being over-comers is terrifying.

Questions to Ponder from Symrna

1. Are we willing to suffer tribulation and persecution? What is our attitude toward suffering and difficulty? Are we quick to compromise and change when we should stand?

2. How do our present priorities and values demonstrate we are prepared to suffer financial loss and proverty for Christ's sake?

3. What has been our response to suffering verbal abuse, false accusation, ridicule, or marginalization from others? (Note: If we are not able to endure this well, then how prepared are we to die for Christ?)

4. How prepared are we to suffer at the hands of Satan? (In the Last of the Last Days, Satan is given power and authority to rule over, hurt, and kill the believers, Revelation 13:7-10).

FIVE

ALERT AND READY: LESSONS FROM PERGAMUM

(REVELATION 2:12-17)

The church of Pergamum was in a difficult place. They were doing good, but they were losing focus. Jesus told them to repent and stop tolerating sin.

Pergamum, a sophisticated city and center of Greek culture and education, boasted a 200,000-volume library that was second only to the famous library in Alexandria in Egypt. Pergamum was the center of four of the most important gods of the day—Zeus, Athene, Dionysus, and Asclepius. The city's chief god was Asclepius, whose symbol was a serpent who the people considered to be the god of healing. People came to Pergamum from all over the known world to seek healing from this god.

Rome granted the proconsul of Pergamum the rare power known as "the right of the sword," meaning that he could perform executions. To the church in this city, Christ described himself as the one who has a sharp two-edged sword (1:16). Just as the sword was a symbol of Rome's authority and judgment, Jesus' sharp, double-edged sword represents God's ultimate authority and judgment. Only Christ has ultimate power over life and death.[1] Whose sword will we fear?

1. Jesus says, "The One who has the sharp two-edged sword says this:" (NASU)

This section starts off with the statement concerning Him who has the sharp two-edged sword. Notice, it is not Satan. Jesus is the One with the sword. What is this sword? Hebrews 4:12 tells us the word of God is a sharp two-edged sword with tremendous power. The Bible is quick and powerful destroying lies and everything that exalts itself against the knowledge of God. It is important to know and to learn how to use this sword in the last days.

This is the same sword that comes out of the mouth of Jesus in the beginning of the book in 1:16. It is the same sword that comes out of His mouth at His Second Coming in Revelation 19:15.

We must consume the word of God (listen to, read it, study it, and more than anything else, obey it). The greatest detriment today as to why we do not consume God's word is our insatiable desire for entertainment. We spend hours on social media, watching TV, movies, and our phones. None of these things prepare us for the end times.

2. Jesus says, "I know where you dwell, where Satan's throne is;" (NASU)

Satan's throne was where Satan dwelt. It is here the saints from Pergamum lived and suffered even to the point of death. Jesus named one person who was a faithful witness to his death. His name was Antipas (meaning "against all") and he died a martyr's death.

We need to be very careful that we do not blameshift our sinful behavior and ungodly choices onto our difficult circumstances. If we are in Christ, then it really does not matter where we live, nor what our circumstances are. Our external situations should be of little consequence to our internal spiritual life. We often make excuses for ourselves that are not excuses at all. Imagine ourselves standing before Jesus explaining why we sinned or compromised or denied Him. It would be impossible to find an excuse good enough to justify these wrong actions or thinking.

3. Jesus says, "You hold fast My name and did not deny My faith even in the days of Antipas, My witness, My faithful one, who was killed among you, where Satan dwells." (NASU)

Just as the Smyrna Christians remained faithful, so also did the Christians from Pergamum. They both were able to remain faithful because their focus was on Jesus.

Four times in this sentence Jesus uses the personal pronoun 'My'. Everything is about Jesus, even their suffering. He commends the believers because amid persecution they stood strong unwavering. They remembered they were suffering for Jesus. This helped them to endure persecution to the death.

If our focus stays solely on Jesus, then we to will be able to endure. We are to hold fast. We must use the strength Jesus has given to us to seize and hold tightly to His faith. It is His faith that will sustain us. It will not be easy, but we can do this.

Jesus says, "My faith" rather than "your faith". Jesus is the author and finisher of our faith. Faith is not ours, but it belongs to Him. God is always the initiator of faith. Only when He speaks can there be faith. We need to always be listening for His voice, and then respond to His voice by believing what He says – this is faith. As humans, we never initiate faith. There is no room for us to arbitrarily manufacture faith. We do not decide about an issue and then God acts. This is not faith; God calls it presumption. Our responsibility is to believe what God says, not believe what we say or want.

4. Jesus says, "But I have a few things against you, because you have there some who hold the teaching of Balaam, who kept teaching Balak to put a stumbling block before the sons of Israel, to eat things sacrificed to idols and to commit acts of immorality. 'So, you also have some who in the same way hold the teaching of the Nicolaitans." (NASU)

This is quite an amazing turn of events. Jesus has just commended the believers of Pergamum for being willing to die for Him, now suddenly there is a rebuke and warning. We must understand that just because we are doing something correct, Jesus does not overlook what wrong we are doing. He commends and He rebukes. There were two disturbing teachings in the church that caused this reprimand. One was the teaching of Balaam and the other was the teaching of the Nicolaitans.

The teaching of Balaam: Balaam was an Old Testament prophet who was covetous. He eventually caused Israel to stumble by his deceit and trickery. He got Israel to eat things sacrificed to idols and to commit acts of immorality, (Numbers 22-24).

The teaching of the Nicolaitans used the grace of God as a license to sin. It involved moral liberties not approved by God. There were two main ideas. If we are in Christ, then we are (1) free to eat foods sacrificed to idols and (2) allowed to be sexually immoral.

(Note: These two teaching are very similar, but the Nicolaitans used the freedom in Christ as the pathway to justify these actions. Balaam's approach was 'if you cannot beat them, then join them'. This approach used pseudo relationships / friendships to create ungodly compromises.)

We know that Jesus wants solid unwavering commitment to the death; but He is just as concerned about what we believe and how we live. The implication is that believing false teaching leads to sinful living. If the teachings that we are holding to allow us to sin, then we know with assurance it is a false teaching. False teachers and false prophets like Balaam use deceit and trickery to convince people that sin is somehow acceptable. In the last days there will be many who fall because of deception.

It is necessary to speak particularly to the sin of Balaam. Balaam encouraged King Balak of Moab to have his people befriend the Israelites, so rather than remaining enemies, they developed ungodly relationships between them. Through deception the Moabites invited the Israelites into ungodly compromise. The result of Balaam's trickery sucked Israel into idolatry and sexual immorality.

There is an important present-day application to this awful story. Instead of the world inviting the church to join them, we have made it worse by the church inviting the world to be part of the church. In an ill-conceived attempt to draw the world into the church, the church compromised its calling. There were two major shifts made by the church. The first shift was the compromise from the Gospel of Jesus to the prosperity gospel. This shift greatly affected the type of teaching and preaching from Christ-centered to that of self-help and feel-good talks. The second shift moved the church away from offensive words like holiness, purity, right / wrong, sin, punishment, hell, and repentance. In place of these words came ideas like God loves you no matter what you do, no one is perfect, God understands, do not judge, accept everyone, the church needs to be more relatable to the culture, and on and on it went.

The church in its effort to be more relatable to the culture has ended up thinking like the culture and, in so many instances, acting like the culture. Sometimes it is difficult to tell the difference in perspectives and attitudes of the world from the church. We have forgotten there is a God who is going to judge the world, both the saved and unsaved. This is rarely, if ever discussed in the church.

We must realize that the Good News of the Gospel is narrow, it is offensive, it is hard, and it is difficult to hear when explained correctly. Changing and modifying the Gospel to make it more palatable and acceptable to the culture has produced a compromised gospel at best and a false gospel at worst.

Jesus was both perfect love and truth. It was because of His truthfulness that the culture crucified Him. Certainly, everyone wants love, but you cannot have God's love without the God's truth. The church too often has compromised by ignoring the hard truth and only speaking of love. The Gospel approach today seems more of a bait and switch approach. In essence, this is fraud. Let us tell the whole truth and nothing but the truth with love.

Just like we have seen in Old Testament times as well as in New Testament early church, the church today struggles with idolatry and sexual immorality. The church today is reeling under the weight of false teachings that give permission for these sins. While most churches do not promote idolatry and sexual immorality overtly, they end up doing so inadvertently by their silence and lack of confrontation on these matters.

Idolatry is materialism promoted through the false prosperity gospel. This false teaching stimulates greediness and encourages covetousness, which is idolatry (Colossians 3:5). In addition, it creates Christians who think they should never have to suffer because God only wants to bless them.

Sexual immorality: is rampant in the church. The statistics reveal that 68% of Christian men have viewed porn within the last month. Even worse, pastors are not that far behind at 50%. This translates that seven out of ten men sitting in church have looked at porn at least once in any given month. For Christian women, the percentage is edging upward past 20%. The church unfortunately is extremely silent about sexual immorality and the reason is because the church has gone soft on sin and does not want to be offensive.

These two sins, idolatry and sexual immorality are the two most destructive of all sins in which we can take part. Both these sins more quickly and more extensively dehumanize us than any other sins. When dehumanization happens, we are no longer able to relate intimately to anyone including God. All relationships become superficial. This topic needs much more discussion, but this is not the purpose of this book. Please take the time to study the following two scriptures: Psalms 115:4-8 and 1 Corinthians 6:16-18.

5. Jesus says, "Therefore repent; or else I am coming to you quickly, and I will make war against them with the sword of My mouth." (NASU)

Repent is the great call in the Last Days. We must change our thinking about God and who He is, and about sin and how destructive it is. God does not and will not tolerate sin. Yes, He does forgive sin, but He also punishes sin. Forgiveness and punishment are not exclusive to one another.

Those who promote and hold to these false teaching will find themselves at war with Jesus. When there is false teaching the whole church suffers. Leaders must discern and teach sound biblical doctrine. We are not exempt from punishment if we are tolerating wickedness and false teaching even if we are doing many good things.

Sin causes even those who are innocent to suffer. For example, Adam sinned, and we all became sinners and are suffering. It much better for the church to judge sinfulness in its midst, rather than have Jesus coming to make war.

The words that Jesus speaks with His two-edged sword to Pergamum are words of punishment and destruction. This is the meek and mild Jesus speaking. He is not for us if we choose sin and self-indulgence over bringing Him honor and glory.

Note: There are Christians who have a wrong belief about Jesus. They falsely believe He is okay with our sins. He is not! God hates sin. His Son died because of our sin. Jesus did not die so we could continue in sin. He died to set us free from sin and that is how He expects us to live – free from sin. The power and freedom of the Holy Spirit does not give us a license to sin.

6. The Pergamum Promise: he who overcomes: (i.e. he who is victorious and who perseveres in the face of conflict and hardship.)

We can eat of the hidden manna and receive a white stone that has our new name written on it. Jesus said He was the manna or the bread of life that came down from heaven in John 6:32-40. Eating of the hidden manna seems to be suggesting that we will always and forever find our sustenance and nourishment in Christ. God who hid Jesus in times past has now revealed Him to us in these last days, (1 Corinthians 2:7-13).

The white stone may be a picture of Christ that was the stone Daniel saw, which destroyed all kingdoms of the world, (Daniel 2:35). In biblical times, it was common that the host would invite friends to an event, such as a wedding by giving a white stone. The white stone was like a ticket allowing entrance into the event. If Jesus has given us this stone, then we have entrance into the eternal kingdom of God.

Questions to Ponder from Pergamum

1. Do I pretend to serve God, but also live to serve myself and my sinful desires? (e.g., Ananias and Sapphira)
2. Is my life one of daily godly sorrow and repentance? How did you come to this conclusion? (Righteousness is proof that shows the fruit of repentance. We stop sinning permanently.)
3. Do I understand that God will not tolerate my choosing to sin? (He will not just fight against me, but He will war against me. (Revelation 2:16))
4. How do I make Jesus my only bread?

SIX

ALERT AND READY: LESSON FROM THYATIRA

(REVELATION 2:18-29)

The church of Thyatira was struggling, but they were improving. Sin and false teachings were a distraction for them. They needed to repent.

Thyatira was a blue-collar town and a center for manufacturing. The city had many trade guilds for commerce such as cloth making, dyeing, leather-working, bronzeworking, and pottery making. Lydia, who was Paul's first convert in Philippi, was a merchant from Thyatira (Acts 16:14). Scholars think it to be the most insignificant of the seven cities, but it receives the longest letter from Jesus.

Christ describes Himself as the Son of God. Jesus is distinguishing Himself from Apollo and the Roman emperor, as people believed they were the sons of the chief god, Zeus. These verses describe Jesus with eyes like a flame of fire and feet like polished bronze (cf. 1:14–15; Daniel 10:6).

Both fire and bronze speak of judgement throughout the Bible. The Tabernacle of Moses show fire and bronze coming together. The bronze altar was where the Israelites sacrificed animals for sin offerings. They would kill an innocent animal, place it on the bronze alar, and then burn it with fire. This was how God judged sin in the Old Testament.

The eyes of Jesus are like a flame of fire. He sees and He looks with judgement. How is He looking at us? What does Jesus see? We can hide nothing from Him, as He sees and knows everything. Should there be habitual and ongoing sin, then He is not kindly smiling at us with loving eyes. Jesus does not ignore sin. [1]

The feet of polished bronze show judgement. Why the feet? It tells us that Jesus will move with action to deal with the sin. He does not idly stand by letting us continue to sin.

God often throughout both Testaments judged the households of faith. We are not exempt from the judgements of God in this life, especially if we are not obeying all that Jesus commanded. It is His kindness to judge us now. If we respond correctly to these mini judgements, then it protects our eternal future, and we will not face the Great White Throne Judgement.

1. Jesus says, "I know your deeds, and your love and faith and service and perseverance, and that your deeds of late are greater than at first. "But I have this against you, that you tolerate the woman Jezebel, who calls herself a prophetess, and she teaches and leads My bond-servants astray so that they commit acts of immorality and eat things sacrificed to idols." (NASU)

Jesus acknowledges the deeds of the Thyatira Christians. They had love, faith, service, and perseverance, even increasing in these godly characteristics. While increasing in these spiritual disciplines this did not negate the problem of tolerating the wrong thing in their midst.

As believers we cannot weigh our good deeds against sinfulness. We often believe by doing the right things it will counteract the one wrong thing we are doing. It is easy to think that the one wrong thing is not that important in relation to all the good we are doing. While God acknowledges the good things we do, it never justifies the wrong that we do. Sinful things are always sinful. Dressing up a sow in a beautiful dress with makeup does not change the fact that it is still a pig.

Jesus knows that by tolerating this false prophetess, she is destroying the church. Already, she is leading people astray. Whatever increase in goodness the church has gained, it will through her teachings vanish.

Over time tolerating evil and wicked people no matter how strong and good the church is, will cause its decline and destruction. As it is true on a corporate level, it is also true on a personal level. Sin always corrupts. The goodness that we have becomes poisoned by the wickedness we tolerate. It only becomes a matter of time for this to become an obvious reality.

This letter mentions another destructive individual. She is the prophetess, Jezebel. While in the Old Testament she was not a prophetess, she controlled 400 prophets of Baal. Most people consider her the most wicked woman in the Bible. Jesus has already mentioned Balaam and the Nicolaitans, but now He adds Jezebel to the list.

It is interesting that the teaching of these three groups centered on idolatry and sexual immorality. Any teaching that actively promotes sinful behavior or allows sinful behavior, Jesus is against. We must not allow ourselves to be deceived by anyone who makes an excuse for sin, no matter who they are.

This church was tolerating false teaching that either excused sin or encouraged the believers to actively engage in sin. The word tolerate can mean to forgive, leave, let it alone or yield up. The church refused to confront her sins. Perhaps, they did not want to offend, or confront or get involved, but these is not an option for Christians.

No one has perfect doctrine or understanding. We are all are in error to some degree. However, there is a significant difference between error and a fundamental departure from the truth. The Christian community today barely understands the doctrine of sin, and as a result this ignorance veers far off course in properly dealing with sin. So many Christians are obtuse to the destructive nature and consequences of sin. They minimize or even scoff at sin as if it is nothing. Others gloss over God's hatred of sin by changing His nature and character. It is important for us to view sin in the same way God views sin.

2. Jesus says, "I gave her time to repent, and she does not want to repent of her immorality. Behold, I will throw her on a bed of sickness, and those who commit adultery with her into great tribulation, unless they repent of her deeds. And I will kill her children with pestilence, and all the churches will know that I am He who searches the minds and hearts; and I will give to each one of you according to your deeds." (NASU)

Jesus was displeased with the Thyatira church because they were tolerating sin. However, He was not quick to bring judgement. It was His desire that they repent, and she repents. Jesus takes no pleasure in judgement, but only does so when there is no repentance.

Even in the face sin, God shows mercy and grace, not because He is tolerant of sin, but because He is giving us an opportunity to repent. We can often mistake God's longsuffering of our sin as proof that He is okay and tolerant of sin. The grace and love of Jesus is wonderful, but not so we can continue in sin (Romans 2:4; 1 Peter 3:8-9, 20). God knows whether someone is willing to repent or not. The wording is critical here. Jesus says, "she does not want to repent" rather than saying, "she cannot repent". As Christians if we do not repent, it is because we do not want to repent. God's grace is always greater than the power of sin.

Jesus said he would throw this Jezebel onto a bed of anguish. Her sin will become her anguish and judgement. Paul, in his first letter to the Corinthian church alluded to this idea. It was concerning the Lord's table and the table of demons. The Corinthians were trying to eat at both tables. The result of this was the member became sick and some died, (I Corinthians 11).

All who were willing participants of her sins would also suffer great tribulation; but even then, Jesus gave hope to the Thyatira church should they repent. The phrase, "I will kill her children with pestilence" refers to those who believed and are practicing her teachings. Jesus cannot allow unjudged sin to remain in His church. A little leaven leavens the all the dough. Allowing sin to remain unjudged in a church is a disaster.

In verse twenty-three there are two inferences to the fear of the Lord. The first inference to the fear of the Lord is "All of the churches will know that I am He who searches the minds and hearts."

Why would all the churches know Jesus searches the minds and hearts. It would be because of the severe judgement that would come upon the Thyatira church.

We cannot hide sin in our minds or hearts. We may be able to hide our sin from others, but we cannot hide our sin from Jesus. Hidden sin is just as destructive to the person as doing it overtly. Jesus is omniscient – He know and sees everything.

The second inference states, "and I will give to each one of you according to your deeds". Jesus will give to each of us according to our deeds. This could be a terrifying thought to us if we are continuing to choose sin. Paul tells the Galatians, "Do not be deceived, for whatever you sow you will reap." Again, this does not mitigate the forgiveness of God, but it does show us that even though God always forgives, He also punishes and rewards us accordingly.

There are no exceptions to this idea of sowing and reaping, and therefore Paul says do not be deceived. We may not connect a specific action to a certain result, but it does not nullify the reality. It makes no difference if we recognize it, see it, believe it, or even refuse to accept this truth. None of these things changes the fact that we will reap what we sow.

3. Jesus says "But I say to you, the rest who are in Thyatira, who do not hold this teaching, who have not known the deep things of Satan, as they call them — I place no other burden on you. Nevertheless, what you have, hold fast until I come." (NASU)

There was a group within the church that did not succumb to the false teachings of Jezebel. So, while there were those in the church that did not agree with her, yet they were still tolerating her. Jesus said to the true believers, "Get rid of her". This was the only responsibility He was giving to the rest of the church. Jesus was not going to require anything else from them. Everything else they were doing Jesus approved of.

The 'deep things of Satan' are teachings that encouraged and allowed sin. Jezebel and her followers taught that these "new ideas" needed special knowledge or insight before they could be truly understood. Thus, these teachings appealed to pride and our other evil desires.

In today's church there is the same problem. There are so many false teachings that people consider to be "new knowledge" or require "special knowledge" to understand. These "new" false teachings are undermining the centuries long doctrines held by the church. Jesus warned His disciples multiple times about this problem. He said, in the last days there will be numerous false teacher and prophets. There has been in the last twenty to thirty years an unprecedented attack on the Bible. In the past, these attacks have been subtle; but recently, these attacks have not been so subtle.

A few of the false teachings today are:

- Excusing and being soft on sin
- Minimizing the consequences of sin because God does not punish the believer
- Redefining what is sin and what is no longer considered sin
- Minimizing the fear of the Lord
- Focusing primarily on the material world (material blessings rather than spiritual blessings)
- Eliminating the reality of hell since it is not really a literal place of eternal punishment
- Dismissing the creation story as poetry or an allegory, so we cannot take it literally

All these false teachings mentioned are extremely dangerous. They weaken the church, and they weaken the believer leaving both unable to manage well in these last days.

4. The Thyatira Promise: He who overcomes, i.e., he who is victorious and perseveres in the face of conflict and hardship is rewarded and keeps (obey) My deeds until the end...

Again, we see the idea of obedience. This is not a 'when we feel like it, we will obey' God's word. It is long-term diligent mindset that we will do all that Jesus commands. "Until the end" tells us this is an obedience that never tires or give us, but it is continual.

Verses twenty-six and twenty-seven are important for a proper interpretation later in Revelation concerning the man-child. "To him I will give authority over the nations; and he shall rule them with a rod of iron, as with a rod of iron, as the vessels of the potter are broken to pieces" Many people interpret the man-child as Jesus in Revelation 12 based on this phrase taken from Psalms 2:8-9. Certainly, it is talking about Jesus, but now we see that it is also talking about overcoming believers. This is a subject that we will address in the third book.

There is an important principle for us to understand in the connection between obedience and authority. Jesus promises eternal authority and rulership to those who obey. The more we obey, the more authority of Jesus we are able use and have.

There are too many Christians who want authority without holiness. This becomes a disaster for the person that has the authority. They will often self-destruct. It is also a disaster to those who are under this type of person, as the authority becomes abusive and destructive.

Christ is our reward. He is our morning star. He is the hope of a new day dawning.

Questions to Ponder from Thyatira

1. Have I been thinking that I am exempt from the judgements and punishments of Jesus? Why or why not?
2. Why is God not content that I am increasing godly characteristics in my life, if I have sin that I am tolerating?
3. What are the two great sins that believers (especially in the Last of the Last Days) need to be aware of? Why are these two sins so significant?
4. How should we reconcile God's discipline and punishment with His forgiveness? Are they mutually exclusive? Why or why not?
5. Is everyone of equal authority in this life and the next life? Why or why not?

SEVEN

ALERT AND READY: LESSONS FROM SARDIS

(REVELATION 3:1-6)

The church of Sardis only had a few believers without soiled garments. Jesus had nothing good to say about them. The were nearly dead spiritually and needed to wake up.

The wealthy city of Sardis had been one of the most powerful cities in the ancient world due to heavy trade among the Aegean islands. Gold and silver coins were first minted at Sardis. The wealth of the city eventually led to moral decadence. The city had become lethargic, its past splendor a decaying memory.

Knowing this church's deeds, Christ had no good words to say. The believers may have had a reputation for being alive, but they were dead. Like the city itself, the church in Sardis may have been trying to live on past glory. They had compromised with the surrounding society to the point that they had become lethargic. They were as good as asleep, so Jesus told them to wake up and repent.

There are recorded five commands focusing on watchfulness in these verses. The city had been sacked twice because the watchmen on the walls had not seen the enemies scaling the cliffs. Thinking that they were impregnable on the mountaintop led to a deadly complacence. What had happened to the city was happening to the church, and it needed to wake up. [1]

1. Jesus says, "He who has the seven Spirits of God and the seven stars, says this:" (NASU)

He is the One who has the seven Spirits of God (Isaiah 11:2). This signifies His deity. In addition, He has the seven stars of God, which are the seven messengers (leaders) or angels of God to the church. This signifies His authority here on earth. Jesus has all power and authority.

2. Jesus says, "I know your deeds, that you have a name that you are alive, but you are dead. 'Wake up, and strengthen the things that remain, which were about to die; for I have not found your deeds completed in the sight of My God." (NASU)

Jesus knows all that the Sardis Christians were doing (or in this case not doing). They were alive physically, but dead spiritually. Jesus warns them to wake up, strengthen what still is for those things are about to die. Their deeds and works were inadequate. God had higher expectations than how they were living.

There are believers saying, "God is not concerned about what we do, but only that we have faith." God is very concerned about what we do as well as our faith. James, in his letter states, we cannot separate works from faith.

Whenever we separate our deeds from our faith, it produces spiritual death. When we make this separation, we become the 'walking dead'. Just as the Christians in Sardis who were true believers, we to can fall asleep spiritually – we can be dead.

What is the primary reason for falling asleep? The primary reason as to why we fall asleep is we tolerate sin (Romans 13:11-14). We tolerate sin rather than trying to eradicate sin. Whether or not we ever eradicate sin from our lives before Jesus comes is not the point. Our heart attitude toward sin is its eradication. We should not look to make a peace accord with sin.

Sin desires to kill us! The pleasure of sin is the anesthesia that keeps us from knowing and feeling the destructive power of sin in our lives. After the anesthesia wears off, we feel the pain from our sin. Sin brings to us fear, shame, and guilt, but rather than repent we hide. Eventually, overwhelmed by our fear, shame, and guilt, we seek out the sin again to anesthetize the pain we created. Ever so slowly we begin to fall asleep.

Jesus says to wake up and strengthen what little spiritual life we have left.

The application here is that those in the city of Sardis felt it was impregnable. They did not have to be alert or ready. So many of us have the same type of attitude. We think that being in Christ makes us impregnable, in that, nothing can harm us not even sin. So, we do not watch or prepare ourselves as we should. As a result, we grow careless about sin, proper values, and right priorities. We do not as the first thing seek the kingdom of God.

3. Jesus says, "So, remember what you have received and heard; and keep it, and repent." (NASU)

Jesus challenges the Christians at Sardis to remember. The order of these two ideas seems reversed, but Jesus intentionally spoke them in this order. There were two things to remember:

- What they had received
- What they had heard

What had they received? They received the kingdom of God and so many other spiritual blessings. Now, because of sin, the Sardis Christians were dead and endangered of losing it all.

What had they heard? After receiving the kingdom, they heard how they were to live in the kingdom.

Sin causes us to easily forget the important things. Forgetting these things creates a lethargic and careless mindset that puts us to sleep (spiritual deadness). We wander about as if lost in the fog.

It is through daily repentance we keep alert and ready for the Last Days and the Second Coming. We must understand what biblical repentance is and is not. It is not crying and saying we are sorry. It is not saying we will never do it again. It is not confessing what we did. It is not remorse. These are good things, but they are not biblical repentance. Biblical repentance is changing your thinking to agree with what God says. If we think correctly, then we will speak correctly, we will believe correctly, and we will behave correctly.

4. Jesus says, "Therefore, if you do not wake up, I will come like a thief, and you will not know at what hour I will come. (NASU)

This is a severe warning. Not knowing when the Master is returning is hugely problematic (Matthew 24:50-51). The only time the Bible uses this phrase, 'a thief in the night' is in relation to the ungodly not knowing of Jesus' return. However, Jesus is now putting these Christians into the same category as the unsaved.

Those of us who are awake, alert, and prepared will not be surprised by the coming of Christ. Jesus will never come as 'a thief in the night' to genuine believers.

5. Jesus says, "But you have a few people in Sardis who have not soiled their garments; and they will walk with Me in white, for they are worthy." (NASU)

There were a few in Sardis who were genuine followers of Christ. These people had not soiled their white garments. The Bible interprets white garments in Revelation 19:8. White garments are the righteous acts of the saints.

We do receive the righteousness of Christ, but He also expects us to live righteously, keeping our garments clean and white. We must not spoil our garments through the mud and filth of the culture. Walking in purity, holiness and righteousness daily is crucial to our ability to remain awake. We must not take part in idolatry or sexual immorality[2] of any kind. Therefore, faithfulness and obedience are of the utmost importance. Soiled righteousness is not acceptable to Jesus. He is not okay with our sins.

When we live righteously before Jesus, we are the ones walking with Jesus. Those of us who walk with Him are worthy of Him. The opposite is also true. Living a sinful lifestyle makes us unworthy to be a follower of Jesus. The Lord cares immensely how we live.

6. The Sardis Promise: He who overcomes, i.e., he who is victorious and perseveres in the face of conflict and hardship is rewarded.

Not only did the Sardis Christians have to wake up, but they also needed to overcome. If they would wakeup and be overcomers, then they would retain their white garments. They would be rewarded accordingly.

In the context of overcoming or not overcoming, there is an important reality to understand. Jesus says, if we overcome, He will not erase our name from the book of life. In those days, the city often had a registry of their citizens. To have one's name erased was to lose your citizenship. If someone died, then there name was erased from the city register. If we are faithful to the end, then we are assured of our eternal state.

The primary context of this verse is that we as faithful overcomers would not have our name erased from the book of life. However, we are left then to ponder the other side of the equation. What if we are not faithful overcomers, but remain asleep?

All overcomers will receive a public commendation from Jesus before the Father and His angels. What a great reward to receive. Jesus says to all in heaven, "Well done good and faithful servant".

Questions to Ponder from Sardis

1. In what ways do I understand that Jesus sees and knows everything that I do, say, and think? How does this affect my life?
2. What is it that causes people to fall into a deep slumber or stop being watchful? What are we supposed to be watching?
3. How do Christians often think about sin and righteousness? What is one reason for being careless and having wrong values?
4. What is biblical repentance?
5. Jesus states, "Blessed are those who are victorious." What sorts of things are we overcoming or having victory over?

EIGHT

ALERT AND READY: LESSONS FROM PHILADELPHIA

(REVELATION 3:7-13)

The church of Philadelphia was the other church that Jesus commended without rebuke or warnings. They understood God's sovereignty, and they were faithfully obedient to the words of Jesus.

The citizens of Pergamum founded Philadelphia as a frontier gateway city to the central plateau of Asia Minor. The earthquake of A.D. 17 that had destroyed Sardis had also been particularly devastating to Philadelphia because the city was near a fault line, and it had suffered many aftershocks. This kept the people in fear, causing most of them to live outside the city limits, away from buildings that could crush them during the numerous earthquakes.

Philadelphia was a small church in a difficult area with no prestige and no wealth, discouraged because it had not grown. Christ had no words of rebuke for this small, seemingly insignificant church, and he described himself to the church in Philadelphia as the one who is holy and true. [1]

1. Jesus says, "He who is holy, who is true, who has the key of David, who opens and no one will shut, and who shuts and no one opens, says this:" (NASU)

The first thing this letter discusses is God's holiness and there is no crookedness in Him. He is truthful and true. God cannot make a mistake. This truth was important to the church of Philadelphia because it felt weak, insignificant, and forgotten.

We all need an understanding of God's holiness and truthfulness. As we walk in these truths, we see an amazing God. It does not matter whether we feel weak, insignificant, or forgotten; He has not abandoned us. God will move on our behalf by opening and closing doors that in our weakness are impossible. (Note: these are not doors we think God should open for us, but doors that God has chosen to open. This verse is about God's sovereign will rather than our will. Most would never choose the doors of suffering. So, even in our suffering, we know it is His will.)

It is impossible for God to change, as He is always true. This truth requires the God of the Old and New Testaments to be the same God. His character, attributes, and nature can never change. This is a great comfort to us, for it means that God is not capricious or arbitrary. He sovereignly and lovingly guides while caring for us.

2. Jesus says, "I know your deeds. Behold, I have put before you an open door which no one can shut, because you have a little power, and have kept My word, and have not denied My name." (NASU)

Note: in these two verses Jesus speaks twice about an open door, which no one can shut. Jesus, by repeating this phrase, wants those of the Philadelphia church and us today to realize that He is the sovereign Lord. He is in absolute control.

Jesus knew the deeds of the Philadelphia church, as He sees all and knows all. Jesus is always aware of their suffering. Even in persecution they did not deny the name of Jesus. These believers were willing to suffer loss and death.

This theme, 'we can hide nothing from Jesus' is all throughout these two chapters. The concept of God's omniscience and all-seeing are extremely important characteristics to meditate on for two reasons. First, it brings us comfort, in that God misses nothing. Secondly, these characteristics teach us the fear of the Lord because God misses nothing.

If we are obeying, then knowing these characteristics about God, becomes a great comfort and blessing. However, if we are living carelessly in disobedience, then these characteristics should put the fear of God in us. Let us choose obedience.

We have extraordinarily little power to make happen what should happen. Our smallness or insignificance is immaterial to God; and therefore, it also should be to us. God works on our behalf not because we are strong and mighty, or clever and insightful, but because we are faithful and obedient.

What does it mean to deny His name? Whenever we compromise, we have denied the name of Jesus. Most often we think only in the terms of verbally denying Christ. In truth, there is more than one way to deny Christ. We can do it by being silent when we should speak up; or we do not stand strong when we should have. We can sign a document denying Christ. Whenever we have chosen to avoid suffering by choosing the easy way, we are denying Christ. Even our actions and attitudes can be a mechanism for showing our denial of Christ. This happens when our sinfulness or ungodly character are so bad no one knows we are a Christian.

In the country where we minister, the government continually pressures Christians to deny Christ in writing. The government tells them to sign a document saying they are no longer going to follow the Jesus way. If they do not sign the paper, then the authorities force the Christians to move out of their village leaving everything behind (lands, houses, possessions, friends, and family). The price for following Christ is destitution but Christ sees all that is happening to these Christians. He sees that they do not deny His name.

3. Jesus says, "Behold, I will cause those of the synagogue of Satan, who say that they are Jews and are not, but lie — I will make them come and bow down at your feet, and make them know that I have loved you." (NASU)

Here the natural Jews are again persecuting spiritual believers. In Revelation 2:9 Jesus says the natural born Jew is no longer a Jew. What does this mean? Jesus confirms Paul's definition of what it meant to be a Jew (Romans 2:28-29). In John 8:39-47, Jesus challenged the natural unbelieving Jews, saying their father is not Abraham, but Satan.

While it is true that there are natural Jews, this ethnic advantage is no longer spiritually any consequence from an eternal perspective. The only advantage now is being in Christ.[2]

Since the crucifixion and ascension of Jesus, God considers His chosen people to be those who are in Christ through faith (1 Peter 2:9-10). No longer is the natural Jew considered to be the true Jew, in God's opinion.

God considers any religion that persecutes the church to be of Satan. All the ungodly will bow before the King of Kings, as well as before the saints. This is the final proof of God's love for us, and it is the saints' vindication.

4. Jesus says, "Because you have kept the word of My perseverance, I also will keep you from the hour of testing, that hour which is about to come upon the whole world, to test those who dwell on the earth." (NSAU)

The Philadelphia church kept the words of Jesus with cheerfulness and hopeful endurance. They remained constant not wavering in their commitment of obedience. It is for this reason God keeps them from the hour of testing. Vincent Word Studies says the preposition 'from' in this case implies the idea of 'in'.

The verb "keep from" is the same Greek verb in the Lord's prayer ("Deliver us from the evil one," Matthew 6:13 NLT). As Jesus said before his death, "I'm not asking you to take them out of the world, but to keep them safe from the evil one" (John 17:15 NLT).[3]

We should not draw a wrong conclusion here. Jesus is not offering an exemption from persecution to anyone, but He is saying, "I will keep you eternally safe in spite of the persecution". Already millions of Christians have suffered and died at the hands of their persecutors since John wrote these words. Nowhere in the Bible is there the promise of not having to suffer persecution. In fact, Jesus has promised just the opposite.

God has limited persecution of Christians to specific areas throughout history. Jesus prophesies of a time when the whole world (believers around the globe) will suffer great persecution at the same time and at the same level of intensity. It will test our perseverance. Millions of us will die and others of us will find deliverance. We see this in idea in Hebrews 11:32-40. There has always been death and deliverance, and we need to be prepared for both.

5. Jesus says, "I am coming quickly; hold fast what you have, so that no one will take your crown." (NASU)

Jesus tells the Philadelphia church He is coming quickly. Everyone has long died since Jesus said this. Their death was His Second Coming, and this may also be the case for us. Whatever happens to us, we must always remain alert and ready, either for His return or our death.

This church has their deeds and perseverance, which Jesus says, "Use your strength to seize these things and no matter what, do not let them go." In doing this no persecutor or devil can take their crown. Revelation 2:10 calls this the crown of life. It is the crown of eternal life. Our eternal life with God is the victors crown that is proof of our perseverance and obedience.

6. The Philadelphia Promise: He who overcomes, i.e., He who is victorious and perseveres in the face of conflict and hardship.

Jesus says, "I will make him a pillar in the temple of My God, and he will not go out from it anymore; and I will write on him the name of My God, and the name of the city of My God, the new Jerusalem, which comes down out of heaven from My God, and My new name." (NASU)

Our greatest reward is to be in God's presence forever and ever. In this relationship, we will find the greatest and deepest satisfaction possible.

Those who overcome need never to worry about losing this relationship as Adam did. He sinned and had to leave the Garden and the presence of the Lord. We will never have to leave the presence of God because we will never sin again.

Jesus will write the name of God on us. We will be His forever. The new Jerusalem in Revelation 21 and 22 speak of the bride of Christ. After the Second Coming we will truly be one with the Lord and we will live happily ever after.

Questions to Ponder from Philadelphia

1. Are there ways I am living in which I could be denying Christ?
2. There is a direct correlation between trusting God and fearing things in life. Fear always reveals a lack of trust. Are there ways I am not trusting God?
3. Am I properly prepared for the Second Coming, no matter whether I may suffer, or Jesus delivers me?
4. Is being with Jesus my highest ambition in life? If not, why not?

NINE

ALERT AND READY: LESSONS FROM LAODICEA

(REVELATION 3:14-22)

The church of Laodicea was the other church about which Jesus had nothing good to say. This church was greatly deceived about their spiritual condition and needed to repent.

Laodicea was the wealthiest of the seven cities. The city was known for its banks, its manufacture of a rare black wool, and a medical school that produced eye salve.

The allusion to the Laodicean water supply is a fitting metaphor for the activities of this church. Laodicea had always had a problem with its water supply. The city of Hierapolis, to the northwest, was famous for its hot mineral springs. An aqueduct had been built to bring water to the city from the hot springs. But by the time the water reached the city, it was neither hot nor refreshingly cool—only lukewarm and filled with minerals making the water taste terrible. According to Christ, these believers were neither hot nor cold; instead, they were merely lukewarm, as bland as the tepid water that came into the city.

Note: Christians have thought that this cold and hot refers to extremes in our spirituality. That is Christ would rather have "cold" people who have no faith at all, rather than "lukewarm" believers who are passive and careless in their faith. So, people have understood the word "cold" to be negative, and the word "hot" positive, and the word "lukewarm" as also negative. However, we should take both "cold" and "hot" as positives. Christ wished that the church had cold refreshing purity, or hot therapeutic value, but it had neither.[1]

1. Jesus says, "The Amen, the faithful and true Witness, the Beginning of the creation of God." (NASU)

Jesus is 'The Amen', which means firm or trustworthy. There is no duplicity in Him. He is the fulfillment of all that God has spoken. He cannot lie, and He does not change. He is the faithful Witness and the true Witness. Whatever He speaks, He does. There is no darkness or shadow in Him. Jesus also says that He is the Beginning of the creation of God, (cf. John 1:1). Jesus is God! While Christ is faithful and true the Laodiceans were not. Jesus is all He says He is. This is our assurance and confidence. There is nothing more that we need beside Him. He is all in all.

2. Jesus says, "I know your deeds, that you are neither cold nor hot; I wish that you were cold or hot. So, because you are lukewarm, and neither hot nor cold, I will spit you out of My mouth." (NASU)

The Laodiceans were not able to hide anything from Jesus. They were totally unaware of their spiritual condition. They were self-deceived. Self-deception comes from hearing the Word and not putting into practice what they heard (James 1:22-24). It is the same for us today.

Jesus decides our spiritual condition based on our deeds and not our personal feelings or intentions. How we live and what we do is significant. The Lord is also telling us that we cannot separate how we live from what we think and believe. If our actions and beliefs are not consistent and compatible with one another, we have self-deception. Our actions and attitudes reveal what we truly believe.

What is it that would make us lukewarm? There are two thoughts. The first thing would be the toleration of personal sin; that is, doing what is wrong or evil. Practicing sin would be the greatest contributor. The second thing would be the lack of doing what is right. We may not overtly sin, but we can sin by omission. The sin of omission is whenever we fail to do what is right. We are responsible to faithfully do what is right. Both these types of sins will cause us to be lukewarm.

Being lukewarm displeases God to the point He rejects us, spitting us out of His mouth. When we go to church on Sunday, read our Bible, pray every day, and do other Christian activities, and choose to live in sin and disobedience to Him, then this is being lukewarm. Doing right things does not negate our toleration of personal sin.

Iniquity takes us from a place of zeal and passion for God and His Kingdom and brings us to a place of coldness and deadness, (Matthew 24:12). If the kingdom of God is not paramount in our thinking and pursuit, then we are lukewarm, (Matthew 6:31). In the Western world materialism distracts so many of us. Today, materialism and consumerism have become the motivation for too many Christians. These things expose greed and covetousness, which the Bible calls idolatry, (Colossians 3:5).

Living in such a materialistic age is a challenge. Let us consider the pressures of our culture and society today. This is not only the reality of Western civilizations, but it is fast becoming true on a global level.

There are worldviews or ways of thinking that have permeated our cultures around the world. These worldviews affect how we think about our lives and our culture. They affect how we act, how we see things, how we talk about things. Three of these worldviews are mentioned in relationship to Laodicea and they are worldviews that impact us today. These worldviews have an asterisk. As we read through these, we need to seriously consider our personal lives. Have these philosophies and ideologies crept into our thinking and behavior? These things definitely keep us from properly being able to remain alert and ready for the Second Coming.

Practical Deism*

We remove God from the centrality of our life, keeping Him at a distance until we decide to invite Him for His help. After He helps us, we send Him back to His far-off relegated place.

Sexual Immorality

Any sexual activity outside of a marriage between a man and a woman is sin. This includes things such as pornography, masturbation, adultery, fornication, homosexuality, and lustful desires in one's heart.

Existential Theism*

Self is central to all things with everything being about me. What self wants, and what self experiences are the most important of all things. Life is about what I feel and think, and every aspect of life self defines. Reality and truth are personally defined by self.

Practical Naturalism*

Material possessions are our most important goal and priority. We measure life and success by solely material achievement. The prosperity gospel is one example of this thinking.

Iniquity /Sin

These are the habitual and intentional sins that we tolerate day after day and year after year. We make little effort to stop and eradicate these sins, but to just live with them and accept them.

Hedonism

This is the pursuit of pleasure and the avoidance of pain. We consider suffering to be evil and contrary to what life should be about. A close cousin to this philosophy is Epicureanism which believes that entertainment and ease are high priorities for this life.

Narcissism

Narcissism is the absolute love of self, even above others. It becomes the worship of self. Self is number one. No one or anything comes before me.

This list showed us seven tremendous pressures (sins) Christians deal with. These pressures squeeze the spiritual life out of us bringing us to a place of being lukewarm. It is a fight to resist and remain passionate about God and His Kingdom over the long haul. These sins are human centric to the core.

The worst thing a human can do is become human-centric. The prevailing humanistic philosophy of the day tells us to love ourselves, but God tells us to deny ourselves. This denying of self is the greatest way in which to properly love yourself.

The chart below shows the digression of a culture that loves itself. It begins in the early 1900's ending at the year 2000. Self-love did not stop in the year 2000, but it has only grown worse and has now become an epidemic. There have been pivotal points in the twentieth history, which moved the focus of self-love along: the Roaring Twenties, the hippy movement of the 1960's, and the infatuation of self at the turn of the century.

- 1920s – Self-indulgence
- 1930s – Self-preservation
- 1940s – Self-delusion
- 1950s – Selfishness
- 1960s – Self-expression; Self experimentation
- 1970s – Self-acceptance
- 1980s – Self-esteem
- 1990s – Self-admiration
- 2000s – Narcissism (self-worship)

Philosophies that indulge self are never a good thing. It takes us down a path we never wanted to go and for longer than we ever expected. Self is insatiable and will always demand more, more than we could ever give.

This is why Jesus says we must die to self. In this way we can be saved from ourselves and truly live.

3. Jesus says, "Because you say, "I am rich, and have become wealthy, and have need of nothing," and you do not know that you are wretched, and miserable, and poor, and blind, and naked." (NASU)

The Laodicean church was a wealthy church. They were proud of the material accomplishments. However, they were neglectful of their spiritual life. These Christians were reflecting the values of the culture around them, rather than reflecting the values of God's kingdom. Their true condition, i.e., their spiritual condition was just the opposite of their material position. The worst thing is that they were unable to see their true spiritual condition.

If we live in a self-indulging manner the result is self-delusion. We are unable to see our true reality and identity. We wrongly think that wealth accumulation and self-sufficiency are the most important goals. We justify these goals saying, we just need a little more, or we are preparing for retirement, or this is something we deserve. In Deuteronomy 8:11-14 God warned the Israelites of this very thing. God blessed the Israelites, and then they forgot Him. We must remember that it is God who gives us the power to gain wealth, and that wealth is for the extension of His kingdom.

Ever so slowly our spiritual life begins to diminish and ever so slowly it ebbs away. Eventually, we have lost our passion and zeal, and so we gradually grow lukewarm. The cares of this world do this to us. So often, we are not even aware of what is happening to us. There is a reason why the Bible calls wealth 'the deceitfulness of riches". In our western cultures today there has never been so much wealth in the history of the world. We must carefully evaluate our life. Is God and His kingdom really the most important thing?

4. Jesus says, "I advise you to buy from Me gold refined by fire so that you may become rich, and white garments so that you may clothe yourself, and

that the shame of your nakedness will not be revealed; and eye salve to anoint your eyes so that you may see." (NASU)

The very things the city of Laodicea was famous for were the very things the church lacked. They were materially wealthy, but Jesus wants them to buy gold refined by fire. The implication here is that the Laodicean church was trying to avoid suffering and persecution. At that time in history if a person were wealthy enough, he could buy himself out of the trouble. God expects us to suffer especially if we are living a righteous life. Jesus prophesied suffering to His followers.

The city was also famous for their black wool, but they did not have white garments. White garments are the righteous acts of the saints. Again, the implication is that they were playing a game with their Christianity. They were "Christians", but were not doing what Christians were supposed to do. They were not living a righteous life.

Finally, the city was famous for their eye salve. They could help others physically, but they could not see their own blindness.

We are needing to buy from Jesus. How do we buy these things from Jesus? The only way in which we are going to get the gold, garments, and eye salve is if we are willing to pay "all" for them. Following Jesus will cost us everything. If we are not willing to suffer loss for the sake of Christ, then we are not willing to pay the price.

This is a strong demand, but this is exactly what Jesus did. He gave up everything in heaven for the sake of the Father's kingdom. The king is expecting nothing less from us. Peter speaks of this suffering in his letter.

1 Peter 1:6-9 {6} In this you greatly rejoice, even though now for a little while, if necessary, you have been distressed by various trials, 7 so that the proof of your faith, being more precious than gold which is perishable, even though tested by fire, may be found to result in praise and glory and honor at the revelation of Jesus Christ; 8 and though you have not seen Him, you love Him, and though you do not see Him now, but believe in Him, you

greatly rejoice with joy inexpressible and full of glory, 9 obtaining as the outcome of your faith the salvation of your souls. (NASU)

Our faith is more valuable than gold the fire has refined. Where is our faith today? Jesus is measuring that faith. It is our faith that will carry us through troubles and trials, not material wealth. All that we have materially Jesus will allow to be stripped away in a moment of time during these last days. Think about it. What will our life consist of if the enemy takes everything away? While we may have nothing material, we will not be miserable, poor, blind, and naked spiritually. We need to make sure that we are right side up seeing things from God's perspective.

5. Jesus says, "Those whom I love, I reprove and discipline; therefore, be zealous and repent." (NASU)

Jesus said several extremely hard and difficult things to the church of Laodicea. His motivation was love and His perspective was eternity. It is not the heart of Jesus to be mean, but He will speak truthfully hard. The motivation of Jesus is always love.

He loves us tremendously and wants what is best for us eternally. Today hard words offend people; they become upset when someone tells them the truth. We falsely believe that no one should ever say something we do not like or agree with. The difficulty with this type of thinking is that the truth is offensive. It is hard and highly confrontive. Therefore, we must humble ourselves under the hand of God and receive His rebukes and reproofs with grace.

We know that we are responding correctly to God's discipline when we become passionate and zealous about God's kingdom, and we also repent of our carless and selfish living.

This letter should cause us to pause and think about how we are currently living our lives. Are we truly living for the glory and honor of God? He wants us to be alert and ready for His Second Coming. He does not want to come to us like a thief in the night. We are children of the day, so we must be aware. The culture wants us asleep and to be as unprepared as they are.

Be zealous for the kingdom of God. Live in God's kingdom as if there were no tomorrow. We must live with a different set of values and priorities. Let us not worry about tomorrow, God knows what we have need of.

Does this sound too radical, too out there? These are actually the words of Jesus to us from the Sermon on the Mount. If we want a truly exhilarating and an unbelievably satisfying life, then we must live on the edge. The world is becoming more radical against God and His ways. We will need to become more radical for God and His ways.

The time short when no man can 'sit on the fence'. The culture will force us to make a choice. If we are moving in the right direction, i.e., with all our hearts toward the kingdom of God, then we will make the right choice. If, however, we are longingly looking back at the material world we are trying to leave behind like Lot's wife, then we will lose everything, even perhaps our spiritual life. Be living salt or become a pillar of salt.

6. Jesus says, "Behold, I stand at the door and knock; if anyone hears My voice and opens the door, I will come into him and will dine with him, and he with Me." (NASU)

He is pleading with us patiently at the door. We do not want to be like the lover in the book of the Song of Solomon, she waited too long to answer. When she got to the door, He was no longer there (Song of Solomon 5:1-7). Jesus will not always stand and knock forever. There is a time and season for each of us. We need to be careful that that time does not pass us by. We need to make ourselves ready and we need to stay alert.

Often this verse is used for salvation regarding the unsaved, but this is not the context of this verse. This verse is speaking to us who have fallen asleep, who have grown careless in these last days. We are the ones who have become distracted with the life of this world. We do not hear Jesus knocking or we are not interested that He is knocking.

Let us quickly open the door. This means we will need to change our lives, and in some cases, drastically. We will need to reevaluate our goals, values, and priorities to make sure they are in alignment with the kingdom of God.

- The Laodicean Promise: To him who overcomes, i.e., he who is victorious and perseveres in the face of conflict and hardship)

Jesus says, "I will grant to him to sit down with Me on My throne, as I also overcame and sat down with My Father on His throne."

There will be a time in the future where we can relax, but it is not in this life. We must remain vigilant, sober minded, alert and prepared now. If we do this right, then we will be able to sit down with Jesus on His throne in victory. We will rule and reign with Him. Oh, what a glorious day that will be!

We will overcome; we will be victorious.

Questions to Ponder from Laodicea

1. In what ways has the letter to the Laodiceans challenged your thinking and belief system?
2. What does my lifestyle reveal about my values and priorities? Are there areas of my life that are inconsistent with God's values and priorities? If so, what are they?
3. How have the seven pressures mentioned in this chapter affected you?
4. If you found yourself reacting to the challenge from Jesus in this letter, why do you think that is?
5. Would you be content with only food and clothes? How did you determine the answer to this question? Is it based on how you are living right now?

Summarization of the Seven Letters:

Mentioned at the beginning of this chapter was the thought that we might find ourselves surprised at the things that Jesus emphasized.

1. Jesus knows and sees everything we do. This includes both our righteousness and our sins. We are to strongly hold onto those things that bring honor and glory to the Lord.

2. Jesus tells us to test spiritual authorities to verify they are true and genuine. We can only do this if we know well what the Bible says, and we understand the nature, character, and attributes of God.

3. Jesus does not allow us to tolerate any sin in our lives. If we tolerate sin in our lives, we will grow cold and leave our first love. Once we identify sin, we must quickly repent and believe what the Lord says. Repentance is agreeing to think what God says and faith is agreeing to believe what God says. This is our work to do.

4. Jesus does not want us to tolerate false teaching or sin in the church. Any teaching that minimizes, ignores, promotes, encourages, or allows sin is false. Beware especially of idolatry and sexual immorality.

5. Jesus challenges us to keep persevering in our trials and persecution. We are not to fear persecution or loss in our suffering for Him. He requires us to be faithful and obedient even to the point of death.

6. Jesus says He will war and fight against those who continue to practice and promote sin. Living sinfully creates lethargy and apathy that eventually causes us to fall asleep. This is extremely dangerous eternally. For the believer Jesus should never come as a thief in the night.

7. Jesus reminds us that we must always have the right values and priorities. The Lord warns us pride is blinding, making it impossible to properly evaluate ourselves. Materialism that produces ease, comfort and convenience is not the right way to measure success.

8. Jesus encourages us, loves us, and comforts us.

9. Jesus tells us of so many magnificent promises to those who persevere, and who are faithful and obedient. We must never give up. We must overcome.

TEN

THE ABSOLUTE AUTHORITY OF THE BIBLE

Ideas About the Bible

What is the Bible? Genuine Christians view this book as God's word to humanity, which we would consider to be absolute and filled with truth. God shares His story of how He relates to all His creation. We can see in precise detail His interactions with peoples and nations. He tells us about who He is and what He wants each of us to be. Throughout the Bible God continually displays His majesty and glory. And on those same pages we see humans continually rejecting or trying to hijack God's glory for themselves.

There are so many ideas and thoughts about the Bible. There are destructive ideas that come from those who are overtly anti-God. However, other negative ideas and thoughts come from so-called Christians bringing into question the authenticity and veracity of the Bible.

Humanity is always attacking the Bible, and we can see this happening throughout history; but now it is being vehemently assaulted. This chapter will be dealing with our perspectives and ideas about the Bible. How do we really view the Bible? Do we take the Bible seriously, or do we view it in a take or leave it manner?

If you were to use the checklist below, which boxes would you mark?

☐ It is the Word of God to humans		☐ It is human ideas about life & God
☐ It is the truth		☐ It is only moral stories
☐ It is the absolute truth		☐ It does have some truth
☐ It governs every aspect of my life		☐ It is filled with good suggestions
☐ It is completely true		☐ It does have some errors
☐ It is the only book in its category		☐ It is like all other religious books
☐ It is for all times and for all cultures		☐ It is mostly obsolete

This checkbox exercise is meant to give us insight into our perspective and thinking about the Bible. It will reveal how we will use or not use the Bible in preparing for the End Times and the Second Coming.

If we checked any boxes in the right-side column, then the Bible will not be the go-to book in our preparation process. The reason for making this statement is because we do not view the Bible as the absolute authority that has absolute truth. Our attitude toward the word of God will decide our willingness to use the Bible in preparing ourselves adequately and appropriately. However, if you chose only the left-side column of boxes, it still does not guarantee that you will use the Bible for your preparation.

What is it that shows we will use the Bible in our preparation process? The biggest factor showing we will use the Bible for our preparation is whether we are currently obeying all that it tells us to do. We do not allow ourselves reasons, excuses, or exceptions as to why we do not obey. We just obey!

The Absolute Authority

Is the Bible the absolute authority for our lives or not? If it is not, what is? There will always be something that acts as the absolute authority for our lives. Why is this such an important issue? It is this authority that informs our values and priorities. We can choose so many different authorities to govern our lives, but only one will properly prepare us for the future.

Whenever we make excuses for not obeying God's word, then we have set ourselves up as the absolute authority. We think that we know better than God. However, we do not know or see the future, but God does. He informs us what to do and how to do it, so we can truly be prepared.

If this is true, i.e., our attitude & approach to the Bible influenced by how we view the Bible), then there are three big questions for us to wrestle with. Is the Bible God's written word to mankind? Is the Bible absolute truth? Is the Bible trustworthy?

How we answer those three questions decides the value you will give to the Bible.

Low Value	High Value
The Bible we ignore	The Bible is the focus of our lives
The Bible we do not read	The Bible we read continuously
The Bible we do not obeyed	The Bible we always obey
The Bible we do not think is relevant	The Bible speaks to every issue

The Bible speaks loudly to the future, our future. If there was a book that could tell us the future, would we devour it or pass it off as unimportant? If that book could tell us exactly what to do to properly prepare for that future would we study it or ignore it? We can read the Bible, and yet still not prepare ourselves for the future. This can happen because we have a negligent attitude toward the Bible that allows us to casually disregard it or to "take it or leave it".

In the first chapter of Proverbs there is a strong warning and stern rebuke given by lady wisdom, (Proverbs 1:20-33). We would be wise to heed her warning by giving serious consideration to what she is saying. The time will come according to her (wisdom) when it becomes too late to avoid future trouble...she will just laugh at those who did not prepare or listen to her.

Properly preparing for the End Times and the Second Coming requires us to believe in the absolute authority of the scriptures. Let us summarize this section as it sets the tone for the rest of this chapter.

- We cannot keep making excuses for not obeying God's word.
- We cannot keep believing that our situation is unique or special, therefore God's word does not apply.
- We cannot keep acting carelessly and negligently towards God's word, (a take it or leave attitude).
- We cannot keep thinking God's word has little value in how to live life.
- We cannot keep saying that God's word is out of touch with culture and reality, therefore making it obsolete and no longer practical.

If these are our thoughts or things we say, then know with certainty that the danger we will meet will have catastrophic and devastating consequences for our future.

The Bible and the Fool

In the Bible, a fool is anyone who resists God or who is in rebellion against God. There is an untold number of people who are in this category of rebellion against God. They are ungodly people who speak lies about God and the Bible.

Often these people are the so-called experts in their fields of study. This negative perspective about or toward God creates a huge problem. They are highly biased against God or the idea of God. Paul, in Romans 1:21-22, states that these types of people, while professing themselves to be wise, have become fools. They may even have educational degrees and be seen as the "expert". However, if they are anti-God or are dismissive of God, then they are fools. Below are five examples.

- Scientists who promote Darwinism and old earth theory (no God)
- Anthropologists / Psychologists who deny sin (everything is a disease or sickness)
- Teachers /Professors who teach relativism (no absolute truth)
- Humanists / Secularists who promote materialism and supremacy of man (man is central)
- False Bible teachers who twist the scriptures about important doctrines.

We need to take great care about listening to these types of people. The lies of Satan have darkened their minds. They love darkness more than light, and their deeds are evil. Therefore, what they say is at best questionable, and at the worst, a lie. These people have an evil agenda.

We must use discretion who we are listening to and discern how we are listening. We cannot look to these people who are anti-God for truth. It is all too easy to change the standard for deciding truth from the scriptures to another source if we are listening incorrectly. It is subtle, and it is extremely dangerous. If we are trying to prepare for Christ's return, but we are using sources other than the Bible, then we will come up short in our preparation.

This brings us to the crux of the matter. We must be determined that whatever the Bible says it is always right. It does not matter who is talking. If what they say differs from the Bible, we must always side with the Bible. This can be difficult to do, but this is what we must do. We must use the Bible as the standard for measuring humans, it is not for humans to measure the Bible.

If we do not decide that the Bible is always correct, then we will find ourselves in the same position as Adam and Eve. We will begin to question what God has said. When this happens, death and destruction are not far behind. If we question the Word of God, then there will be doubts and a lack of confidence in the Word. This will cause us to subconsciously dismiss the Word.

No one can prepare for the future thinking in a double-minded manner. Either God's Word is always true, or it is never true. Trying to walk on both sides of the fence is impossible.

What is the Bible all About?

The Bible is all about God, His glory, and His honor. This is not only the central idea of the Bible, but also the primary theme of the Bible. It is unfortunate so many Christians view the Bible as a story about humans. It is this idea of mankind starting interactions with God that shows a humanistic approach to the Bible. We put ourselves as the initiators and God as the responder. God is always the initiator and mankind is the responder. We are only able to experience God because He first engages us. Our experiences are on His terms, not ours.

The Bible is first and foremost God's story about Himself, an autobiography. Throughout the Bible, over and over God displays His majesty and glory to us. It is man's response to God's honor and glory that becomes the problem. This began with Adam and Eve in the Garden of Eden. They despised God's honor and glory by trying to gain it apart from God through sin. This horrible response to God's honor and glory continues through the whole Bible until the very end.

All through the Bible there are stories of men and women responding correctly and humbly to God's honor and glory. We can see these right responses in such people as Noah, Job, Abraham, Isaac, Jacob, Joseph, Moses, Joshua, the various judges, Samuel, David, Daniel, Esther, Ezra, and Nehemiah. However, so much of the Bible is a sad commentary on man's rejection of God, and the disdaining of His honor and glory.

The Bible begins with the story of the Creator demonstrating His honor, glory, power, and majesty in creation. In the same manner the Bible ends with the story of Jesus' return to earth in honor, glory, power, and majesty. From cover to cover the Bible is all about God, His glory, and His honor.

Whenever we do not honor God, this causes us to fall far short of His glory (Romans 3:23). This is the essence of sin, not honoring God properly. Our perspective becomes twisted and confused and we think things we should not. We begin to live self-focused and self-centered.

- We define truth and reality to fit our desires.
- We keep God distant until we need His help.
- We believe that God exists for our convenience.
- We think it is God's responsibility to keep us happy and blessed (materially).
- We look at God as an old-fashioned grandfather who is out of touch.

What have we done? We have created a different and lesser god than the true God of the Bible. Then it is easy for us to replace our created false god with something or someone we believe will deliver more and better. Now, we are no longer in a safe place. We have moved ourselves onto the proverbial 'slippery slope' that will not be able to sustain us in these last days.

There are three things that happen to this sort of person. (1) Our expectations increase for an easy and comfortable life. (2) Contentment decreases into great disappointment and dissatisfaction. (3) We consider pain and suffering as evil and avoid them at all cost. When this happens to us, we are unable to prepare ourselves for the days to come. The world and the things of the world have become more important and desirous, even more than God Himself. We are no longer interested in pleasing God, but only in pleasing ourselves.

If God's honor and glory is not our highest goal, then we will sink into the abyss of self. Interestingly, self does not take good care of self. A word picture would be that of a three-year-old trying to take care of himself. He does not know how or what to do, but he only does what is convenient, easy, and comfortable for himself. He will become malnourished, weak, and in grave danger.

Only God can truly take care of us in the correct manner, and He can only do that if we are seeking His honor and glory first.

Mirror, Mirror on the Wall

Mirror, mirror on the wall, who is the fairest of them all?

You have heard the story, I am sure.

"Thou, O Queen, are the fairest in the land," said the mirror.

Then one day, the mirror said to the queen, "Snow White, O Queen, is the fairest of them all."

Well, Snow White became the object of the queen's hatred.

The queen could not stand to have someone fairer than she.

This is, however, the way that we as Christians view the Bible. We use it as a magic mirror. What does this mean?

We use the Bible in a manner that makes us feel good about ourselves. For example, we will select verses that never challenge us or never point out our faults and sins. When we use the Bible in this manner, it then has become our magic mirror. We look at the mirror and tell it to speak something wonderful to us or about us. Whenever we read a verse or passage that says something less flattering, then we despise the mirror and the message of the mirror. We will say, "It is broken, there is no way God would ever say that about us."

At times, we never pick up the mirror. We are too fearful of what it might reveal about us. Still others of us look into the mirror, but we just disregard what is on full display. We think that it could not be talking about us – the mirror is confused. There are so many wrong responses to the mirror (the Bible). The truth of the matter is the Bible is not a magic mirror and we should never use it as such.

No, it is not so much fun to attend to the mirror that affirms things about us that make us blush, that causes us to lose our self-esteem, or that creates trauma in our self-identity. The Bible's reflection of us, while painful is necessary. We need to look closely and carefully at what it is showing us about ourselves. We can ill-afford the luxury of the mirror offending us because it was too much in our face.

James warns us about improperly handling the mirror.

James 1:22-25 {22} But prove yourselves doers of the word, and not merely hearers who delude themselves. 23 For if anyone is a hearer of the word and not a doer, he is like a man who looks at his natural face in a mirror; 24 for once he has looked at himself and gone away, he has immediately forgotten what kind of person he was. 25 But one who looks intently at the perfect law, the law of liberty, and abides by it, not having become a forgetful hearer but an effectual doer, this man will be blessed in what he does. (NASU)

The mirror will always show us who we really are, whether we like it or not. The mirror is always truthful. When we hear the hard truth, we do not like it. We want to quickly put the mirror down, forget what it said, and walk away without changing. However, when we do this, we deceive ourselves thinking we are something different or better than what the mirror told us. So, we end up living life in a fantasy world that we have created for ourselves. There is no escape from this fantasy world except through listening to the mirror of truth. The mirror does not hate us; it is just being truthful. It is the truth that sets us free. It is only the truth that can prepare us for the End Times. A lie cannot offer preparation.

Also, we need to be careful what mirrors we are looking at and listening too. There are mirrors that distort truth. We may have experienced them at a car(NIV)al or fair. These deceptive mirrors make us look different. If you think you are too thin, there are mirrors that can make you look wider. If you feel you are too wide, then there are mirrors that can make you look thinner. If you feel you are too tall or too short there are mirrors that will gladly compensate for whatever shortcoming you have. The obvious problem with these mirrors is they are lying mirrors or mirrors of distortion.

In the same way false Bible teachers are these deceptive mirrors. They use the Bible (the true Mirror) and bend it, and shape it, and twist it in ways that make us feel better about ourselves. They introduce false understandings about sin, hell, man, and God. In the last days there will be so many false teachers, prophets, and apostles. If we do not know the scriptures well, then we could easily become intrigued with the distorted mirrors. If we do not like the true mirror, we will gravitate toward the false mirrors.

2 Timothy 4:3-4 {3} For the time will come when they will not endure sound doctrine; but wanting to have their ears tickled, they will accumulate for themselves teachers in accordance to their own desires, 4 and will turn away their ears from the truth and will turn aside to myths. (NASU)

There is no other book that can tell you the future like the Bible. There is no other book that can tell you how to prepare for that future like the Bible. It does not just tell us about this life, but it also tells us about the next life, and even how to prepare for that life. A wise person will listen to what the Bible has to say, and then actually do what it says to do.

The Right Mentality:

There is a right way in which to approach the Bible, and there is a wrong way. If we do not approach the Bible with a sense of humility, then we will miss what the Word so desperately wants to give us. The Bible wishes to give us an abundant life[1], but this can only be true if we obey it. It takes humility to be obedient.

We can approach the Bible as a wise person, a simpleton, or a fool. God gives us this choice. We decide!

The wise person is a person of humility, and carefully listens and intensely observes.

- After listening to and observing the Truth, we make an informed decision to obey the Word. Thus, we were able to avoid all the negative consequences that come from poor and sinful decisions. We can fill our life with joy and peace by the choices we make to obey. The best preparation for the future is being a wise person.

The simple person chooses to learn by experience.

- In this case, we suffer the consequences of a poor or sinful decision. After we suffer the pain of our choice, then we decide to obey. The problem with this type of approach is that we introduce unnecessary pain and trouble into our lives. So many of these consequences are severe and long-term, which we could have avoided had we decided to choose the way of wisdom. If we are this person, then we are ill-prepared for the future.

The fool is a person who never learns.

- We keep on making the same poor and sinful decisions repeatedly. We blameshift onto others or our circumstances never taking responsibility or ownership for our choices. Our troubles only increase along with frustration and confusion. We never learn from our poor and sinful choices. This person is not at all prepared for the future and will only suffer more.

The Bible, if handled and received correctly, will transform the mind. If we do not transform our minds, then our minds will become conformed to the culture's values and priorities. Should this happen, we will suffer greatly.

The next thing we need to consider is the inclusiveness of the Bible. There are believers who think that the Bible is quite narrow in its application to our lives. Nothing could be further from the truth. The Bible should be informing every area of our life. It is meant to be the filter through which we pass all meaningful decisions connected to Truth.

These areas of life include God, family, self, health, agriculture, economics, work, eating, stewardship, relationships, arts, government, church, education, civics, character, morality, ethics, priorities, goals, and values, to only mention a few. We must allow the Bible to speak to every part of our lives.

If we are excluding the Bible from various parts of our lives, then we are setting ourselves up to not be prepared. We cannot think it is acceptable to be prepared in some areas of our lives and not others. This only means that we are not prepared.

Finally, our approach to the Bible is to view what God says to us as mandates. We cannot think of them as just only suggestions or good ideas. It is God's heart and desire to save us from sin, death, and Satan. If we are not going to obey the Bible, then we will suffer greatly. We must resolve in our hearts to obey. So, no matter how difficult, how hard, how great the sacrifice needed, or how long it takes, we will obey.

Questions to Ponder:

1. Consider carefully what boxes were checked at the beginning of this chapter? Were any of the choices a surprise? Is what was chosen genuinely what is lived? (There must always be a comparison made of the answer given to what is practiced – there should never be a dichotomy.)
2. What is the attitude when reading and studying the Bible? Is it done with sincerity, or is it viewed as more of a Christian duty?
3. What excuses are made for a lack of obedience?
4. How does one know if the word of God is the highest and greatest authority? What is the response and thinking towards the Bible when a so-called expert disagrees with what the Bible says?
5. How does one know if what is practiced and believed is done for the honor and glory of God?
6. How is the word of God used? Is the Bible used to only to generate positive feeling about self, or is it used as a tool that

continually challenges current thinking, attitudes, values, and priorities?

In conclusion, we must make sure that our thinking about the Bible agrees with what the Bible says about itself. The Bible has proven itself over and over. There are enough fulfilled prophecies in the Bible showing it to be divinely inspired and correct. There are no valid excuses for not believing what the Bible says.

There is one thing extremely important to understand. The Bible's focus is Truth. This is its foremost and primarily concern. It is far more concerned about Truth than facts and information. However, its facts and information are truthful and accurate. A successful life from God's point of view is not based on how many facts or bits of information we have. Nor does God measure success on years of education. Should we have a PhD and know little Truth, then that life will not be successful from God's perspective. God does not measure success by knowledge, education, fame, or wealth, but by faithfulness and obedience to His Word.

Choose wisely to whom and to what you listen to.

ELEVEN

A BIBLICAL THEOLOGY OF SUFFERING

The topic of suffering is not at all appealing. The very idea of suffering is repulsive, but why? When God created the universe and everything in it, He said, "It is good, and it is very good". God did not create the world broken. It was perfect! There was no sin, sorrow, pain, or suffering. Adam and Eve rebelled against God and the consequences of that disobedience brought into the world death and destruction. God created us into a perfect world. We were not meant to suffer. Therefore, we struggle so much with suffering because it works contrary to our original created nature.

The punishment of sin is death, suffering and destruction. So, while death is a punishment, it was also God's mercy to mankind. Death would be our escape from this fallen and broken world, but only if we find ourselves in Christ. In the same manner, suffering is also God's mercy to us. It is when we are suffering that we find ourselves crying out to God and drawing near Him. We would have complete disinterest in seeking God, and we would destroy others and ourselves quickly without suffering and pain. It is pain that keeps us from self-destruction.

Suffering requires us to think carefully. Depending on our response to suffering, we will either grow into becoming more like Christ or shrivel into despondency and bitterness. Obviously, we want to become like the Lord, but this is only possible if we respond in godliness to our suffering.

There are three "why' questions we need to answer in this chapter. (1) Why are there people who can endure an unbelievable amount of suffering, survive, and even bounce back? (2) Why is it at the same time, others succumb to great despondency with a little amount of suffering? What makes the difference between the two? (3) Why is this topic even important, and what does it have to do with the End Times and the Second Coming?

What makes the difference between those who are able thrive in suffering and those who cannot? To endure suffering and even thrive during it, we must have a theology of suffering. Any theology of suffering helps immensely. A wrong theology of suffering is far better than none.

When we consider the topic of suffering, there are three basic groups of people. We will view each one of these to see how each group thinks about suffering.

- Those who have no theology of suffering.
- Those who have a non-biblical view of suffering.
- Those who have a biblical view of suffering.

No Theology of Suffering:

The culture of the Western world in general does not create a theology of suffering. This is what happens in a secularist, hedonistic, narcissistic, and materialistic culture that has a worldview of no God. There is no room or meaning for suffering in this sort of worldview.

It is ironic that this is the case. Neo-Darwinism is an evolutionary ideology that underpins so many western civilizations, which base forward movement and improvement on natural selection and survival of the fittest. There is tremendous suffering in this ideology so it should provide a base for suffering, but it does not. In these cultures, man is god, and the major goal is to create a temporal utopia. This ideal utopia has no room for suffering. For example:

- No poverty – everyone shares the wealth equally
- No ill-health – advancement in medicine will solve diseases and sickness
- No divisions – everyone will share the same goals, values, and priorities (even if it is forced)
- Equality of value – because we are basically good, a little education will solve all social problems
- Earth is the Garden of Eden – no waste, no pollution, very green

This list of utopia conditions could continue for pages, but it is not the point of this book. Obviously, one of the primary goals of this worldview is to eradicate all suffering, especially personal suffering. In this ideal, the human collective can bring all cultures and societies to the place of world-wide utopia.

The secularist living with a materialistic worldview, perceives problems and suffering as something to buy himself out of (providing he has sufficient means), or find a way to fix it, or make it go away. If these options are not available, then ignoring or denying the suffering is acceptable, but this can only be done through some sort of medicating. The idea of embracing and valuing suffering is ludicrous to this mindset.

If removing suffering in life is a prime objective, there is no need to develop a theology of suffering. However, suffering is inevitable and those who have not developed a theology of suffering are unable to endure suffering when it occurs. They are unable to cope with life's difficulties, and as a result completely fall apart and breakdown.

Any stressors become mountainous and overwhelming. Fear, worry, and anxiety increase off the charts. There is the sense of a loss of control, so anger and frustration grow in unmanageable ways. Life becomes unbearable. This is what happens when there is no theology of suffering.

To bring this point home we can use a current example, in which people are unable to cope with stress and frustration. It is impossible to have a meaningful conversation in which there is even small disagreements in ideas or opinions. Differing ideas create stress. Therefore, there can be no disagreements. We will not allow anyone or anything to create stress in our lives. As a result of such thinking, we have adopted a cancel culture. Now there is the social media elimination of all perceived threats. This elimination mentality will only continue to grow. People so desperately seek a life of ease, of comfort, and of convenience at all costs.

Unfortunately, many Christians have adopted this same mindset from the culture in which they live. Some western churches have promoted this type of thinking. These false teachers and false preachers promote 'no suffering' through their prosperity gospel. They say things such as, God does not want you to suffer, God promises you only health and wealth, and if you have sufficient faith, then you can name it, and claim it, blab it, and grab it. The world is yours...take what you will.

False teachers also say, "You will not have problems and suffering if you have sufficient faith." These false teachers and false prophets promise a spiritual 'get out of jail free' card that exempts their listeners from any kind of suffering. Not only do you not have to suffer, but they also promise you an overabundance of blessings. So, whenever there is suffering, these believers become ladened down by a sense of false guilt and shame. They wrongly think, "If I just had more faith, then all these problems would not happen to me."

This false teaching does not permit one to develop a robust and biblical coping mechanism for dealing with suffering. Erroneously, these believers have been made to think that suffering has no benefit or value for the Christian life. Just like non-Christians, they also become overwhelmed by their suffering; and in the worst-case scenario they walk away from God, disillusioned.

Non-biblical Theology of Suffering

There are many different views on the theology of suffering throughout the world. There are differences and nuances in these different views, but there are other good books that deal with those things. The purpose of this book is not to discuss them in detail, but to give a general understanding as to what people believe.

The non-biblical theology of suffering does not understand suffering in the biblical context. These cultures have developed a theology of suffering based on their worldviews, but they are not robust. Most cultures throughout the world have a theology of suffering that creates a coping mechanism. However even a wrong theology of suffering is better than no theology of suffering.

There is an attitude in the majority of the world that suffering exists and avoiding it is not possible. This is unlike those who have no theology of suffering and who believe mankind can eventually defeat suffering. In one sense both these perspectives are true from a Christian viewpoint, but not at the same time. There is unavoidable suffering now, and in eternity we will live in utopia.

The various non-theistic worldviews state life is filled with suffering and life itself is suffering. This suffering is all around, creating the expectation that all peoples are going to suffer. One of the results of this understanding is the development of fatalism. That is, whatever will be will be. It is going to happen, and there is nothing that can be done about it. There is a sad purposeless resignation toward the idea of suffering.

In addition, these worldviews do not give a great deal of thought as to why there is suffering and where suffering originally comes from. The majority world cultures place the blame for ongoing suffering on the human condition of desire and ignorance rather than on rebellion against God.

These worldviews have no empathy and compassion for those who are suffering. There is no meaningful help from outside of ourselves in dealing with suffering. Everyone is just on their own.

In summary, what helps people suffer is the idea that they are going to suffer and that it is unavoidable. Thus, they are resigned to it. This thinking allows them to cope with suffering, but not in a robust manner. Everyone is alone in their suffering, and if we could be rid of our desires and become properly educated, then we might have utopia.

The Biblical Theology of Suffering

There are a great many ideas about suffering even among Christians. It is important to understand what is necessary to have a biblical view of suffering. What does God say about suffering? Our own opinions and ideas do not matter, but only God's perspective. There are three aspects of suffering we need to understand. (1) Everyone suffers, even innocent people. (2) There is a biblical way in which we are to manage our suffering. (3) We will find a life in Christ where there is no suffering.

For the Christian it is easy to acknowledge suffering. We understand that God did not create the world with suffering in mind. It was not God's intention for humans nor the rest of creation to suffer. Adam and Eve rebelled against God and in their rebellion brought sin and death into God's creation.[1] This rebellion is the sole source of suffering.

The reason there is so much suffering in the world is because of the first sin. So now, even if we are 'innocent' in a general sense from wrongdoing, we still suffer. This feels so very unfair. Why would a loving God ever allow such a thing? Choice is the issue, and this choice is always a test of love and loyalty. God wants His creation to love Him because they choose to love Him. We are not to blame God for all that is wrong, as it was His human creation that brought onto ourselves all the ills of life. It is like the man who murdered his neighbor even though he did nothing wrong, and then blamed the dead neighbor for dying.

Suffering is unavoidable as long as there is sin. Adam and Eve brought brokenness into world, so now we all live in the broken world.[2] Now we all suffer, but we do not suffer alone. God allowed Himself to be drawn into human suffering, even though He was innocent. He chose to suffer with us and during our suffering gives us hope.

Not only does God suffer with us, but He also empowers us to suffer well. He does not always remove the suffering, but He always gives grace to us in our suffering. We see this in played out in 2 Corinthians 12:7-10. Paul is suffering a problem, and he wishes for deliverance from it. He has been praying for its removal. After three times God finally says to Paul, "My grace is sufficient for you". God is telling Paul that He is not going to remove the suffering. His suffering as well as all suffering have purpose. In another example, Jesus in the Garden of Gethsemane asked the Heavenly Father to remove the cup of suffering (the cross) if possible. It was not possible, and Jesus the Son of God died a gruesome death.

God allowed His own Son to suffer, not so we could be exempt from suffering here on earth, but so we would not have to suffer eternally. The way of the cross is suffering. There is a requirement to pick up and to embrace our suffering.

Since we cannot avoid suffering, then should we choose fatalism? No, of course not! Fatalism is uncontrollable events with no purpose. In Christ, all suffering is under the control of the Father and has purpose. If suffering has purpose, then it also has value. We do not have to have a resignation toward suffering, but instead, we can genuinely engage and embrace suffering. This is uniquely a Christian perspective. Below are examples of the benefits in Christian suffering.

- Suffering reminds us that all is not well and deliverance from it is our hope, (Romans 5:2-5)
- Suffering has a purifying effect, (1 Peter 4:1)
- Suffering gives us endurance and strength, (James 1:2-4)
- Suffering pain from sin informs us not to sin again, (1 Peter 4:1)

We should not think it strange that we are suffering. False teachers and false prophets who teach and prophesy away suffering are lying. Yes, it is true that God wants to and does bless us with eternal blessings, but it is also equally true that God brings us into places of suffering as a means for us to grow, purify ourselves, and draw closer to Him.

1 Peter 4:12-13 {12} Beloved, do not be surprised at the fiery ordeal among you, which comes upon you for your testing, as though some strange thing were happening to you; 13 but to the degree that you share the sufferings of Christ, keep on rejoicing, so that also at the revelation of His glory you may rejoice with exultation. NASU

It is the normal Christian life to suffer. If we are suffering for the sake of Christ, then it is an opportunity to rejoice. Should we be suffering for our sinful choices, then it is an opportunity to repent. If we are suffering through no fault of our own, then it is an opportunity to learn.

We desperately need God's perspective about suffering. For us not to be overwhelmed in our suffering, we must have the right understanding of suffering. How do we think about suffering? Is our view of suffering more humanistic or is it godly? Below is a table that contrasts two views of suffering. Prayerfully consider how we honestly think and believe versus 'what is the right answer'.

Human View of Suffering	God's View of Suffering
As Christians, we should not have suffering in this life.	God has called us to suffer for Jesus. Philippians 1:29; 1 Peter 2:20-21
When living in God's will, we should experience few hardships.	We must go through many hardships to enter the kingdom of God; we were destined for trials. Acts 14:22; 1 Thessalonians 3:3.
Suffering implies something is wrong. It is an abnormal state.	Suffering is normal and inevitable in the Christian life. 2 Timothy 3:12.
Suffering has no redeeming value or positive results.	God uses suffering for our good, to conform us to the likeness of His Son. Romans 8:28-29.
Suffering means that we can have little or no joy and our choice to rejoice is taken from us.	We have opportunity to rejoice in our suffering. Matthew 5:12; 1 Peter 1:6-7.
If God really loves me, then He will put a hedge of protection around me, so terrible trials do not enter my life.	He did not prevent His own Son from suffering, Romans 8:32. He did not prevent Paul, Peter, John the Baptist, Job, and others He loved from suffering.
Spiritual people do not hurt emotionally when they suffer.	Spiritual people feel painful emotions when they suffer, Mark 14:33-34, 2 Corinthians 2:4
When we suffer, this means that God is angry and is punishing us.	Suffering may be God's loving discipline for our own good, Hebrews 12:7-11.

As believers, we would know the right answers to the test above, but there is another test we can take. This next test will challenge us at a deeper level. Do we have a humanistic perspective about suffering? What happens when we are suffering? Check the boxes that apply. Do we...

- Complain about our situation and suffering
- Think life is unfair because we are suffering
- Resent having to endure suffering
- Look to blame someone for the suffering
- Experience fear, worry and / or anxiety about our suffering
- Question God's love, willingness, or ability to deliver us from suffering

These two tests reveal our theology of suffering, and if we find ourselves answering incorrectly in agreeing with the human view of suffering or checking any of the above 6 boxes, then we know our theology of suffering is not biblical. If there are areas where we did not do so well, then we need to repent.

What happens when there is a mixture of humanistic ideas and biblical ideas of suffering? Any mixture of humanism and Bible results in spiritual weakness. Humanism is unable to support the enormous weight of suffering; and therefore, is unable to sustain us in our suffering. These two approaches to suffering for the Christian are philosophically diametrically opposed to one another.

How should we, as Christians, who have a biblical theology of suffering think? We should think in the following manner. There are six basic ideas we need to adopt into our Christian life, so we can be well prepared the End Times and Second Coming.

- We are to have a thankful heart toward suffering, knowing as we respond biblically to suffering it is working a Christ likeness in us.
- We understand that if Jesus suffered, then we will also suffer. The servant is not greater than his master. We believe it is a great honor to suffer.
- We rejoice in our suffering, knowing it is working an eternal weight of glory on our behalf.
- We turn our faces and hearts toward God, asking and knowing He will give us the grace and courage to suffer. We can pray for its removal, but we are more than willing to suffer for the sake, honor, and glory of God.
- We allow our faith and trust in Jesus to grow deeper. As this happens, we will find rest, peace, and joy. We will not suffer in fear, worry, or anxiety.
- We never doubt God's love, care, or ability in our suffering, but we can patiently endure suffering while showing the fruit of the spirit.

What are the implications if we find ourselves bewildered by our sufferings? Do we begin to question the nature, character, and attributes of God? What do these questions reveal? These questions reveal that we do not know the true God of the Bible, but we have instead created a false god. We have created a god in the Bible that does not exist. In our human thinking it is incomprehensible that the true God of the Bible would allow me to endure pain, let alone lead me into it.

All throughout the Bible we see godly men and women suffering. We are not exempt from a life of difficulty. All those who follow Christ will suffer. This is something that Jesus promised us. We must begin to stand strong in the face of it.

We see God leading Joseph to Egypt. It was a great time of suffering for him. He lost everything in one day and became a slave. Later Joseph acknowledge that it was the hand of God.

Genesis 50:20 "As for you, you meant evil against me, but God meant it for good in order to bring about this present result, to preserve many people alive. NASU

The time was extremely hard for Joseph, but he understood God meant it for good. Suffering is hard and God knows this. He is not requiring us to enjoy the suffering; but we can rejoice in it if we keep the right heart and perspective.

There is the story of Job. Again, we see God leading Job into pain and suffering. God took full responsibility for what happened to Job. In Job we see God giving Satan permission to harass Job taking everything from him except is life and wife. Job 2:3 is a telling verse, in which God says to Satan, "Have you considered My servant Job? For there is no one like him on the earth, a blameless and upright man fearing God and turning away from evil. And he still holds fast his integrity, although **you incited Me against him to ruin him without cause**." NASU

There is no doubt this is one of the more difficult passages in the scriptures. We see that God is taking full responsibility for Job's sufferings. As believers we must stop trying to create a God that we feel comfortable with and fits our concept of a nice benign God. He is outside of our box and His ways are incomprehensible. We must allow God to be God and be okay with Him being God. We will never understand Him. This is one of the great truths that make Him who He is.

The greatest example of suffering in the Bible is that of Jesus. He, being perfect without sin, suffered. Jesus is our example, showing us how to endure in tribulation. Since we are disciples of Jesus, then we can also expect the same. The disciple is never greater than the master. This means we are not exempt from suffering.

How do we go about developing a biblical theology of suffering? What are the principles that will undergird us with strength as we move through affliction? These are just a few of many.

(1) How we understand and engage in suffering is critical. Affliction is a human experience introduced by God, and we cannot avoid it while sin exists. When suffering comes our way, we must be willing to embrace it. This embracing is a willingness to walk through our troubles with the right heart and mind, which is exemplified by thankfulness and rejoicing. We are thankful because God is with us during our suffering, and we rejoice that through suffering we are becoming more like Jesus.

(2) All suffering has an eternal value when responded to in a godly manner. Often it feels as if the suffering is only temporal and has no benefit or reward. Thinking wrongly about affliction and trouble only makes life miserable, confusing, and meaningless. We must see eternal value and benefit to it. To do this there needs to be quiet contemplation and reflection about the pain. We cannot allow the suffering to distract us. If we lose our eternal perspective, then we will lose the benefit the suffering brings to us. Paul says it beautifully in second Corinthians.

2 Corinthians 4:17-18 {17} For momentary, light affliction is producing for us an eternal weight of glory far beyond all comparison, 18 while we look not at the things which are seen, but at the things which are not seen; for

the things which are seen are temporal, but the things which are not seen are eternal. NASU

(3) We cannot allow fear into our suffering. Certainly, these times are not enjoyable; it hurts and is painful. The human tendency is to seek an escape and to be fearful. Fear and the strong desire to escape become fertile ground for horribly wrong and sinful decisions. All fear-based decisions lead only to greater difficulty. There is no such thing as noble fear...all fear is sin. God's grace is sufficient for us if we allow it to be. The other great problem with fear is that it grows. Fear is insatiable, so we can never just manage or minimize it. Fear is unrulily; so, we must eradicate it.

(4) God's grace allows us to sit in our suffering, while it does it deep and mighty work.

Romans 5:3-5 {3} And not only this, but we also exult in our tribulations, knowing that tribulation brings about perseverance; 4 and perseverance, proven character; and proven character, hope; 5 and hope does not disappoint... NASU

James 1:2-4 {2} Consider it all joy, my brethren, when you encounter various trials, 3 knowing that the testing of your faith produces endurance. 4 And let endurance have its perfect result, so that you may be perfect and complete, lacking in nothing. NASU

We see that suffering is extremely beneficial in producing strength of character. While escape is the human tendency, we need to adopt a spiritual mentality of remaining. What is at stake here is our trust in the Lord. Do we truly believe that He has our best interest at heart? Do we trust Him? Our ability and willingness to patiently endure our suffering is directly linked to our willingness to trust God. There is no need to trust God if we understand and things are easy. It is when we sit in our suffering that we must learn to trust the Lord.

(5) What should be our motivation when we are having to endure suffering? The great motivator is the honor and glory of God. No matter what is happening to us, we must always keep this in our focus. This dynamic will

sustain us even in the direst of situations. We can draw strength from this truth – all for the glory and honor of God.

Questions to Ponder:

1. Was this chapter distressing? If so, why was this the case?
2. What were some attitudes and thinking about suffering before reading this chapter?
3. What idea in this chapter was the most difficult to accept? What idea was the most shocking?
4. When reviewing the chart about suffering, what side was more predominant or was it more a mixture of both?
5. What happens when there is mixture of a humanistic idea of suffering and a biblical idea of suffering?

TWELVE

THE FEAR OF THE LORD

One of the great truths of the Bible that prepares us well for the End Times and Second Coming is the fear of the Lord. Without this truth working in our hearts, we will find it impossible to remain alert and ready over the long-haul. Our human nature naturally drifts toward carelessness and laziness.

A soldier does not diligently guard the perimeter of the camp because he loves his commander. No, he is diligent because he fears his commander and the consequences. He knows that falling asleep when he should be awake is a personal disaster for him.

If we think for a moment that the fear of the Lord diminishes our love for the Lord, then we do not truly understand either one. These two truths work together in tandem rather than against each other. Both truths are absolutely necessary for a vibrant Christian life and relationship with God. The reason for discussing the fear of the Lord is because of the tremendous neglect and misunderstanding of this truth and its importance in these last days.

The balance between God's love and the fear of the Lord is so skewed that it turns the love of God into a mushy, gushy experience that is not biblical. To minimize or eliminate one of these truths is to destroy the other. It is imperative to grasp what God says about both love for God and fear of God.

Is He Safe?

C.S. Lewis' celebrated children's book, *The Lion, the Witch, and the Wardrobe,* tells of the adventures of four children in the magical kingdom of Narnia. The story is fun, but it is also an allegory of Christ and salvation, with Christ represented by the lion Aslan. When in Narnia, the children meet Mr. and Mrs. Beaver, who describe the mighty lion to them.

Mrs. Beaver said to the children. "If there's anyone who can appear before Aslan without their knees knocking, they're either braver than most or else just silly."

"Then he isn't safe?" said Lucy.

"Safe?" said Mr. Beaver. "Don't you hear what Mrs. Beaver tells you? Who said anything about safe? 'Course he isn't safe. But he's good. He's the King, I tell you."[1]

Today we are no different than Lucy. We want a safe God, a God who is predictable and one who is not surprising in the least. Thus, we create gods with whom we are comfortable with, and feel safe with, and gods we can control.

David McCullough in his book *Mornings on Horseback* tells this story about young Teddy Roosevelt: Mittie (his mother) had found he was so afraid of the Madison Square Church that he refused to set foot inside if alone. He was terrified, she discovered, of something called the "zeal." It was crouched in the dark corners of the church ready to jump at him, he said. When she asked what a zeal might be, he said he was not sure, but thought it was probably a large animal like an alligator or a dragon. He had heard the minister read about it from the Bible. Using a concordance, she read him those passages containing the word ZEAL until suddenly, very excited, he told her to stop. The line was from the Book of John, 2:17: "And his disciples remembered that it was written, 'The ZEAL of your house hath eaten me up'" People are still justifiably afraid to come near the "zeal" of the Lord, for they are perfectly aware it could "eat them up" if they aren't one of His. Our Lord is good, but He is not safe.

David McCullough, Mornings On Horseback

Of any doctrine in the scriptures there is none that is more foundational to living life properly before God than that of the fear of the Lord.

There is a move afoot to redefine, minimize or remove the idea of the fear of the Lord from Christendom. One approach is to directly attack the idea by saying the fear of the Lord is not for today - all we need is love. Another tactic is to redefine the idea into a benign concept of only respect and reverence. Still another method is that of negligence. By never promoting or teaching the fear of the Lord we soon forget it. Why do we treat the fear of the Lord in this manner?

The primary reason for redefining, minimizing, or removing the fear of the Lord is because it has been redefined, minimized, and through practical Deism removed God. The fear of the Lord no longer fits the false god we have created. The two ideas are now in great conflict with one another. Rather than see the true God through the lens of scripture, we have morphed Him into our own vain imaginations.

The ramifications of creating this "new god" are beyond comprehension, as we will discuss in this chapter. One cannot even properly love God if we do not first fear God. Without the fear of the Lord the only alternative is gross and rampant idolatry.[2]

The following article addresses one aspect of this issue quite nicely.

"The first reason why the fear of God is not important for Christians in the United States today springs from the way in which many Christians view God: something akin to a benign grandfather to do favors for us, but then ignore him when convenient. This god is comfortable, easygoing, reasonable, and predictable. This god does not make difficult demands of us, does not ruffle our feathers, and pretty much leaves us alone on a daily basis. He bears absolutely no resemblance to Rudolf Otto's *mysterium tremendum*[3]; as this god has been fully domesticated, tamed, and declawed. In short, this god is an idol, a god who is just like us, a god before whom we do not take off our shoes, a God before whom we need not bow our heads."[4]

There are some who react strongly about having to serve and be in a relationship with a God they must fear. They say, "Who would ever want to follow a God that demands He should be feared"? People are looking for a 'nice' God; that is, a God who is only gracious and kind, never demanding or hard. However, a thorough reading of the scriptures clearly shows a God who does demand that we fear Him.

A.W. Tozer said, "The greatness of God rouses fear within us, but His goodness encourages us not to be afraid of Him. To fear and not be afraid-that is the paradox of faith."[5]

One time many years ago, the king of Hungary found himself depressed and unhappy. He sent for his brother, a good-natured but rather indifferent prince. The king said to him, "I am a great sinner; I fear to meet God." But the prince only laughed at him. This did not help the king's disposition any. Though he was a believer, the king had gotten a glimpse of his guilt for the way he had been living lately and he seriously wanted help. In those days it was customary that if the executioner sounded a trumpet before a man's door at any hour it was a signal that he was to be led to his execution. The king sent the executioner in the dead of night to sound the fateful blast at his brother's door. The prince realized with horror what was happening. Quickly dressing, he stepped to the door and was seized by the executioner. He was dragged pale and trembling into the king's presence. In the agony of terror, he fell on his knees before his brother and begged to know how he had offended him. "My brother," answered the king, "if the sight of a human executioner is so terrible to you, shall not I, having grievously offended God, fear to be brought before the judgment seat of Christ?"[6]

There is a thought that endeavors to explain the idea of the fear of the Lord by separating servile fear and filial fear. In this case, is servile fear has to do with punishment from God because there is an improper or lack of relationship with God. Filial fear has to do with the son or daughter who is in relationship with God but who does not want to offend Him. In some ways this sounds good and does offer a relatively safe way in which to approach the fear of the Lord.

However, the problem is twofold. First, this sort of separation does not exist in the scriptures. It completely removes the idea of punishment for those who do wrong even though they are God's children. The thinking is those who are in God's family are not or should not be punished for wrongdoing. This concept is not in the Bible. God punished Israel multiple times for disobeying Him, even though they were His chosen people.

What are we to do with the passage in Hebrews that is speaking to us (God's children)? These verses specifically tell us that God disciplines and punishes us.

Hebrews 12:4-6 {4} In your struggle against sin, you have not yet resisted to the point of shedding your blood. 5 And you have forgotten that word of encouragement that addresses you as sons: "My son, do not make light of the Lord's discipline, and do not lose heart when he rebukes you, 6 because the Lord disciplines those he loves, and he punishes everyone he accepts as a son." NIV

These verses tell us clearly what God does to His children. He trains us up, educates us, and disciplines us, and He punishes us. Notice God's motivation for punishment. It is love. We dare not eliminate God's punishment; for if we do, we also eliminate His love. To say that God does not punish for sin is contrary to what the Bible declares.

It is equally true that we do not need to fear punishment if we have not sinned. God is not capricious or arbitrary. However, if we are choosing to live in continuous, blatant, and rebellious sin, then beware. God is also patient, and He is not quick to punish; but He does punish, He must punish.

Exodus 34:6-7 {6} And he passed in front of Moses, proclaiming, "The Lord , the Lord , the compassionate and gracious God, slow to anger, abounding in love and faithfulness, 7 maintaining love to thousands, and forgiving wickedness, rebellion and sin. Yet he does not leave the guilty unpunished; he punishes the children and their children for the sin of the fathers to the third and fourth generation." NIV

God is slow to anger and He forgives. However, His forgiveness does not equate to no punishment. For example, a parent forgives a child (not holding their wrongdoing against them), but many times there is still a discipline or punishment that comes.[7] We need to be careful we do not quickly dismiss how God truly interacts with us. There is an over emphasis on God's love to the point that we compromise His righteousness.

God loves and disciplines His children, of this the scripture is clear.

Throughout the Old Testament God was continually disciplining and punishing Israel for their failings in following Him wholeheartedly. The book of Judges brings this idea out most clearly. Israel would follow God for a season, and then begin the process of backsliding. Whenever they reached a certain point, then God's patience would run out and He would send other nations to harass, destroy and bring them into captivity. This happened multiple times. After God subjugated Israel in severe oppression to their enemies they would repent. Then God would relent and send deliverance.

Job is another example of God's discipline. This story is a bit confusing. Job had done nothing wrong to deserve the type of treatment that he received from the Lord. Job even feared God and shunned evil. What more could God ask for?

Job 1:1 In the land of Uz there lived a man whose name was Job. This man was blameless and upright; he feared God and shunned evil. NIV

As the story continues Job complains to God. He wants an audience with God, because he believes that God is treating him unfairly.[8] Job believes that God is disciplining or punishing him for something he did not do. Job is correct in one sense, in that, he is a God-fearing man who was blameless and upright. However, God was not punishing him, but God was bringing discipline to Job, as God often does to all of us.

Job, even though he was a good and upright man, is under the discipline of God. How can God justify this? If we compare eternity to the temporal, the eternal is of much greater importance to God. This means that God will sacrifice our temporal comforts to bring us greater eternal blessings. This is a difficult concept to accept.

There is a difference between discipline and punishment. As parents, we discipline our children in many ways that should not be consider as punishments. For example, we put them on a schedule, this is a discipline. We give them chores to do, this is a discipline. Our children go to school and learn to sit and pay attention, this also is a discipline. Discipline helps children mature and take on added responsibilities well. The more they mature the more privileges and rewards they receive.

Punishment on the other hand has to do with disobedience. Whenever we disobey, God punishes us. Galatians chapter six explains this clearly. God always punishes, and He always forgiven.

God blessed Job in his temporal world. He was the greatest of all the men in the east. God was more interested in Job's eternity than all the temporal blessings He gave him. Job's eternal life was not danger, but God wanted Job to have more blessing in heaven. In all that he suffered, he did it well. God was well-pleased with Job. So, we see God will engage us at times in surprising and hard ways for the sake of our eternal blessings.

God finally reveals Himself to Job. He asks Job about seventy questions and never answers any of Job's complaints. Job realizes that he has misspoken about God and had no right to complain about how God treated him. He throws his hand over his mouth and says...

Job 40:3-5 {3} Then Job answered the Lord: 4 "I am unworthy — how can I reply to you? I put my hand over my mouth. 5 I spoke once, but I have no answer — twice, but I will say no more." NIV

In God's presence, Job no longer focused on his pain and suffering. Even though he believed he had been treated unfairly, his response was that he was unworthy in the presence of a holy and righteous God.

This is really an important point.

There are times when we do not get what we want, what we feel we needed, or we feel unfairly treated by God. What is the solution to this dilemma? We must understand that we are under the discipline of a loving Father who cares far more about eternity than we do. He is lovingly helping us refocus our values and priorities. God wants us to make eternity a higher goal than it currently is in our lives. He will during these difficult times engage us and reveal Himself to us. When we encounter Him during these times it brings everything into proper focus.

As we walk in the path of suffering, we should never speak an accusation against God. At no time should we ever call Him into question about what He has done or is doing.[9] God is good all the time and He never makes a mistake. Our difficulty is in how we define good. The definition of good for us is whatever is easy, comfortable, and convenient in the temporal. However, God's definition of good is whatever matures us into Christlikeness and benefits our eternal well-being. It is here where the conflict is. It is between what we think and what God thinks.

It is our responsibility to respond in a godly fashion and be submitted to His working in our lives whether we agree with it or think it is right. Let us consider what Jesus says.

John 15:1-2 {1} "I am the true vine, and my Father is the gardener. 2 He cuts off every branch in me that bears no fruit, while every branch that does bear fruit, he prunes so that it will be even more fruitful. NIV

Notice what it says. If we are already bearing fruit, the Father prunes us so we can bear more fruit. This certainly summarizes the story of Job. God was pruning Job so he could bear more fruit. In God's economy more fruit is more important than temporal comfort. It can be called pruning or another we can call it discipline. Whatever the case, it was a painful and horrible experience for Job.

We must be very careful not to remake God into the safe and comfortable God that we want. Our minds and thinking cannot remake God nor change God. He is immutable. However, we must change our thinking to agree with who the God of the Bible is. This is where the change must happen.

God is unfathomable. He is infinite in every way. We want a God who works within the confines of a god-box we have constructed. Whenever we do this, we are only creating a lesser god. He can never be the sort of God that fits nicely into the miniscule god-box our vain imaginations that we have created.

Questions to Ponder:

1. As Mr. Beaver is talking to Lucy, what does he means when he says, "Who said anything about safe? 'Course he isn't safe. But he is good. He's the King, I tell you."? (Conflict between not safe and good.)
2. How should Christians think about the fear of the Lord? Why

should it be considered important? Is it necessary or relevant for today? Why or why not?

3. A.W. Tozer said, "The greatness of God rouses fear within us, but His goodness encourages us not to be afraid of Him. To fear and not be afraid-that is the paradox of faith." Do you agree with this idea? Why or why not?

4. What are the theological problems, if any, with separating filial fear and servile fear when discussing the fear of the Lord?

5. The story of Job is at best unnerving to us who read it. If Job is not safe, who is safe? Discuss the story of Job.

6. Why do we tend to create a god who is not a biblical God?

Defining the Fear of the Lord (Hebrew and Greek definitions)

There are many defining ideas as to what the fear of the Lord is. What do the original languages tell us about the fear of the Lord?

In the Hebrew language there are three words that are translated to mean reverent fear, terror, or dread, or simply fear. There are other words in Hebrew for mere respect, reverence, or honor.

In the Greek language the word is translated as fear/terror. Reverence or honor on the other hand uses a different word.

As we can see there is a strong emotional aspect of literal fear involved in this concept of the fear of the Lord. Removing this emotional characteristics of fear and only thinking of it as reverence and honor is to remove the core aspect out from the fear of the Lord. God is far too big not to induce literal trembling and shaking.

There are other words in both languages that can be used to convey the ideas of honor, respect, and awe should have God wanted to communicate that. Let us not be too quick to remove fear from the fear of the Lord. A holy fear is a righteous and good thing.

In the Old Testament as well as the New Testament there are so many stories that combine the idea of literal fear along with honor, respect, and awe for God. The fear of the Lord is a combination of both. Below are three stories to illustrate this point.

(Exodus 19 & 20)

God tells Moses to prepare to meet God on Mt. Sinai. When God comes down to the mountain there is shaking, loud noises, fire, and clouds. The people are warned not to come near the mountain. When all of this happened, the people were terrified. In the end the people told Moses to go and speak to God without their involvement.

(Number 16)

God opened the earth and swallowed up Dathan and Abiram, their families and everything they owned. The people who saw this did not just stand around and think, "Wow that was something?" They were terrified and ran away in great fear. At the same time God sent fire out from His tabernacle and burnt up 250 men, the followers of Korah. The people were terrified of God and His holiness.

(Acts 5)

Ananias and Sapphira, who were struck down and killed for lying. It says all those who witnessed the death of Ananias a great fear came upon them. When his wife, Sapphira also died, it says a great fear came upon the church and everyone who heard about the event.

In these three stories it was God who evoked this fear because of what He did. God has no problem whatsoever in us genuinely fearing His greatness and wrath. These stories illustrate that the fear of the Lord is not just a polite form of awe and respect, but it includes literal fear. We should fear the God who can destroy both body and soul in hell (Matthew 10:28).

The fear of the Lord is not just an Old Testament thought, but this same idea carries into the New Testament as well. God does not and cannot change. He is still the same God in both the Old and New Testament. In our desire for a "nice God" we have morphed Him into something different in the New Testament from the Old Testament. Doing this creates a false God.

Questions to Ponder:

1. Is it possible to linguistically separate the fear of the Lord from the emotion of literal fear? Why or why not?
2. When God showed His glory and majesty or did a supernatural miracle what were the responses throughout the Bible? Were they only respect and awe or was there literal fear involved?
3. What are other examples in the Bible that show the fear of the Lord?

The Story of Adam and Eve

Let us consider another aspect of the fear of the Lord. We see this dynamic played out in the story of Adam and Eve.

Genesis 3:1-11 {1} Now the serpent was craftier than any of the wild animals the Lord God had made. He said to the woman, "Did God really say, 'You must not eat from any tree in the garden'?" 2 The woman said to the serpent, "We may eat fruit from the trees in the garden, 3 but God did say, 'You must not eat fruit from the tree that is in the middle of the garden, and you must not touch it, or you will die.'" 4 "You will not surely die," the serpent said to the woman. 5 "For God knows that when you eat of it your eyes will be opened, and you will be like God, knowing good and evil." 6 When the woman saw that the fruit of the tree was good for food and pleasing to the eye, and also desirable for gaining wisdom, she took some and ate it. She also gave some to her husband, who was with her, and he ate it. 7 Then the eyes of both of them were opened, and they realized they were naked; so, they sewed fig leaves together and made coverings for themselves. 8 Then the man and his wife heard the sound of the Lord God as he was walking in the garden in the cool of the day, and they hid from the

Lord God among the trees of the garden. 9 But the Lord God called to the man, "Where are you?" 10 He answered, "I heard you in the garden, and I was afraid because I was naked; so I hid." 11 And he said, "Who told you that you were naked? Have you eaten from the tree that I commanded you not to eat from?" NIV

There are two aspects about the fear of the Lord shown in this story. One is positive and the other negative.

For a time, Adam and Eve feared God. This was even before they sinned. We are able to know this because they were obeying God. Solomon connects fearing God and obedience to God's commands.

Ecclesiastes 12:13-14 {13} The conclusion, when all has been heard, is: fear God and keep His commandments, because this applies to every person. 14 For God will bring every act to judgment, everything which is hidden, whether it is good or evil. NASU

Proverbs 16:6 By lovingkindness and truth iniquity is atoned for, and by the fear of the Lord one keeps away from evil. NASU

The fear of the Lord that Adam and Eve had before they sinned enhanced their relationship with God. It drew them closer to God. This was a good and holy fear. It did not an inhibitor their relationship. The fear of the Lord is positive. It keeps us from sin and doing what is evil and wicked.

One day, they decided to disobey God, which means they chose to no longer to properly fear God. After Adam and Eve disobeyed, they feared God in a different way. They were now afraid of God in a very negative way.

However, when we do not practice the fear of the Lord in the correct manner another more sinister fear enters the relationship. This can be seen in Genesis 3:10.

Genesis 3:10 He answered, "I heard you in the garden, and I was afraid because I was naked; so I hid." NASU

This fear is the type that destroys and weakens relationships. We want to hide because we are now afraid. It separates us from God and one another.

The point here is that there will always be some sort of fear in our relationships with God. It will either be the fear of the Lord (godly and healthy) or we will be fearful of the Lord because of our sin (ungodly and unhealthy). We choose.

If we truly fear God, then we will fear nothing else. This is a good test for us to see if we really fear the Lord. The fear of the Lord is the inverse of all other fears. If we fear failure, then we do not properly fear the Lord. Should we fear what others think or say about us, then we do not properly fear the Lord. A good, strong, biblical, and healthy fear of the Lord will release us from all other fears.

The fear of the Lord can be taken to the very end of time and on into eternity. In Isaiah 11:1-5 is a Messianic scripture that speaks of the various spirits that will rest on Jesus. One of these spirits is the Spirit of the fear of the Lord. The thought here is the fear of the Lord is not temporary and limited to only earth.

We will either voluntarily fear the Lord, or we will be fearful of Him, (Cf. Revelation 6:14-17). There is a stern warning to humanity by Jesus in the Gospels, (Luke 12:4-5). If we choose not to fear the Lord in this life, then there will be great fearfulness at the Great White Throne Judgement. Everyone will fear the Lord in some manner.

The fear of the Lord is not a suggestion, or a proposal God submits to us for our approval. God does not want us to verbally endorse this idea. He wants it to affect our lives. The fear of the Lord is a commandment, a directive, and a demand of God. It is a doctrine to be lived out and practiced in the manner that He demands, and according to the characteristics He requires.

Questions to Ponder:

   1. How does Adam's sin show a lack of a true biblical fear of God?

2. Why does a fear of God diminish the wrong types of fears?
3. When we fear God improperly what do we as humans tend to do?
4. Do you agree or disagree with the statement, 'there will always be some sort of fear in our relationship with God'? Why or why not?

Love for God and Fear of God

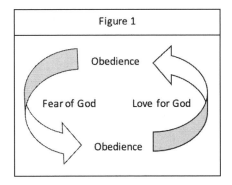

It is important to understand from a biblical view the interaction between our love for God and the fear of the Lord. They are in no way diametrically opposed to one another, but are in fact, complimentary and interdependent to one another. There is a movement afoot in the church today to remove the fear of the Lord. People are wrongly thinking that there is something sinister and twisted about fearing the Lord, but nothing could be further from the truth.

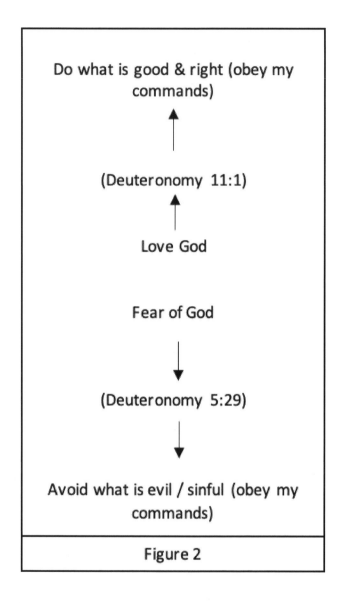

Figure 2

The fear of the Lord creates an internal environment within in us, which makes it much easier to love God and our love for God makes it much easier to properly fear Him. These two great doctrines are at the core focused on the same thing, obedience (see figure 1).

There is another way in which to view these two dynamics. If we love God, then we are motivated to do what is right. In the same manner if we fear God, we are motivated to avoid what is evil and sinfully (see figure 2).

Together, they create the perfect balance for healthy obedience. Disconnecting them or trying to eliminate one hurts the other. They are both absolutely necessary for a life that will be truly God-honoring.

The primary emphasis in today's culture is to love God rather than fear Him. But is this a correct emphasis and approach? What does the Bible say about these two ideas? We may be shocked to discover the emphasis of the Bible.

A comparative quick study of these two ideas is revealing. There are only sixteen verses in the Bible that directly command us to "love the Lord". That seems amazingly low for as much as this subject is discussed. There are a little over one hundred verses that speak of our need and responsibility to love God.

On the other hand, there are between two hundred and fifty to three hundred scriptures that discuss and command us to fear God. As one can see, this is no small topic in the Bible. When compared to loving God, the fear of the Lord is a much greater subject. So, why is the emphasis so much on love?

Solomon said it best in his book Ecclesiastes.

Ecclesiastes 12:13 Now all has been heard; here is the conclusion of the matter: Fear God and keep his commandments, for this is the whole [duty] of man. NIV

What is being said here? Obviously, there is the direct thought to fear God, but Solomon also says, "keep his commandments." Jesus in the New Testament interpreted what this means in the book of John.

John 14:15 "If you love me, you will obey what I command. NIV

It is not strange to combine these ideas together (love, obey and fear of God). The first time these words are used together is in the Old Testament, the book of Deuteronomy. It is as if Moses was explaining what it means to obey God's commands.

Deuteronomy 10:12-13 {12} "Now, Israel, what does the Lord your God require from you, but to **fear the Lord your God**, to walk in all His ways and **love Him**, and to serve the Lord your God with all your heart and with all your soul, 13 and to **keep** the Lord's commandments and His statutes which I am commanding you today for your good? NASU

The fear of the Lord and love or God are equal in their importance and application and should never be pitted against one another. Either truth alone will eventually lead us to a distorted view of God negatively affecting our relationship with Him.

The result of over emphasizing the love of God is we will tend to do what is right, but not forsake what is evil or wrong. Isaiah deals with this issue in the first chapter. In verses 2-9 Isaiah describes the rebellious attitude of Judah. Then in verses 10-20 he suddenly talks about how they are making their offerings and sacrifices faithfully to the Lord. However, God is angry with their hypocrisy.

This was the problem: while they were doing the right things "spiritually speaking" they were also doing the wrong things "practically speaking". They were going to church, singing the songs, reading their Bibles, tithing, and doing all of these "spiritual" things that God had commanded; but at the same time, they were taking advantage of the widow and the fatherless, committing fornication and adultery, filled will malice and backbiting, and not trusting God.

God does not approve of this sort of living. Simply put, we must do what is right, but we must also stop doing what is sinful.[10] It is the fear of the Lord that makes this our reality. There is no cosmic scale, in which God weighs your good and bad deeds; so, if your good deeds outweigh your bad deeds, then you are good to go. This is what all other religions teach. This is not

Christianity. Throughout the Major Prophets and the Minor Prophets the message resounds, "There is no fear of God."

Jim Elliot said: "In reading the Scriptures I find a great moral power. Therein am I made aware of two great forces for good in human experience: the "fear" of God and the "grace" of God. Without the fear of God, I should not stop at doing evil; the fear of God restrains from evil. Without the grace of God, I should have no desire to approach positive goodness. The one is a deterrent from evil; the other an encouragement to good."

The fear of God is to be united with the love of God; for love without fear makes men remiss, and fear without love makes them servile and desperate (J. Gerhard).)[11]

Questions to Ponder:

1. Why does there seem to be a greater emphasis on loving God than on fearing God in our culture today? Does this tend to lead to a healthy Christianity? Why or why not?
2. Where is the fear of the Lord and the love for the Lord supposed to lead us to?
3. Where does the scripture put greater emphasis? Is it on fearing God or loving God?
4. What is the consequence when one truth is over-emphasized improperly over another?
5. Should there be a greater emphasis on the fear of God as opposed to loving God? Why or why not?
6. In much of Christian culture today there is in vogue the 'cosmic scale', in which God weighs my good deeds and my bad deeds. Why is this wrong thinking? (Hint: throughout the scriptures it is understood that bad deeds nullified good deeds.)

Holiness, Worship, and the Fear of the Lord

It is difficult to separate the biblical ideas of true worship, holiness, and the fear of the Lord. The lesser fear of the Lord we have the shallower our worship will be.

In western Christianity, some expressions of worship today are nothing more than an exercise in self-validation. In recent years it has become more common for the central theme of a song to be mostly about me, myself, and I. Other songs are so vague it is difficult to discern the subject. These songs create confusion about who we are really worshipping.

The following is an article written by John MacArthur, titled "Whatever Happened to the Fear of the Lord?"[12]

"How would you react if you were suddenly face-to-face with God?" When Isaiah saw a vision of God, he fell prostrate before Him and cried, "Woe is me! For I am undone." Isaiah felt his guilt and shame in the presence of a holy God. MacArthur reminds us that "We ought to be shaken to our roots when we see ourselves against the backdrop of God's holiness. If we are not deeply pained about our sin, we do not understand God's holiness at all."

Today we often think of the Lord in friendly, pleasant, and passive terms. However, never do we see this in the Bible. The testimony of Scripture is clear: All sinners—even strong believers with mature faith—are right to cower in the light of God's holiness.

For example:

- In Genesis 18 Abraham confessed in the presence of God that he was dust and ashes.

- Similarly, Job said after his pilgrimage, "I have heard of You by the hearing of the ear; but now my eye sees You; therefore I retract, and I repent in dust and ashes" (Job 42:5–6).

- Ezra 9 records the high priest's profound sense of shame as he came before the Lord to worship.

- Habakkuk had a vision of God's power and majesty, and his knees began to knock: "I hear, and my body trembles; my lips quiver at the sound; rottenness enters into my bones; my legs tremble beneath me" (Habakkuk 3:16 ESV).

- In Isaiah 6:1, Isaiah describes how he saw the Lord sitting on a throne, high and lifted up. He heard the seraphim cry back and forth to one another in antiphonal response, "Holy, Holy, Holy, is the Lord of hosts, the whole earth is full of His glory" (v. 3). God's holiness fills all—even when it is hidden from our view.

As Isaiah perceived the holiness of God, he cried out: "Woe is me, for I am ruined! Because I am a man of unclean lips, and I live among a people of unclean lips; for my eyes have seen the King, the Lord of hosts" (Isaiah 6:5).

Some might think that Isaiah did not have a particularly good self–image, that he was not thinking positively, that he was not affirming his strengths. Surely, Isaiah knew that he had the best mouth in the land! He was a prophet of God! He was the foremost spiritual leader in the nation. And yet he cursed himself. Why?

The answer is noticeably clear. We find it in the words "My eyes have seen the King, the Lord of Hosts." Isaiah had seen a vision of God in His holiness, and he was absolutely shattered to the very core of his being by a sense of his own sinfulness. His heart longed for purging.

Perceiving God's Holiness and Our Sin

When we see God as holy, our instant and only reaction is to see ourselves as unholy. Between God's holiness and humanity's unholiness is an immeasurable gulf. And until we understand the holiness of God, we can never know the depth of our sin. We ought to be shaken to our roots when we see ourselves against the backdrop of God's holiness. If we are not deeply pained about our sin, then we do not understand God's holiness at all.

Without such a vision of God's holiness, true worship is not possible. Real worship does not rush into God's presence unprepared and insensitive to His majesty. Worship is life lived in the presence of an infinitely righteous and omnipresent God. We are overwhelmed by His holiness and we are overwhelmed with our unholiness. We may never have a vision of God like Isaiah, but nonetheless, the lesson to be learned is when we enter the presence of God, we must see Him as holy.

Has God become almost human, so affable, and ordinary that we do not understand His holy indignation against sin? If we burst into His presence with lives unattended by repentance, confession, and cleansing, we are vulnerable to His holy indignation.

The Response to Jesus

It is difficult for Christians today to rid themselves from the idea that Jesus was only a passive, amiable, meek–and–mild being who walked through the world making people feel good. We can read stories of Jesus on earth when people were afraid of Him. In fact, it might be fair to say that whenever someone stood face to face with Jesus coming to a true understanding of who He really was, the normal reaction (from believers and skeptics alike) was fear.

The disciples were fearful when they faced squarely the reality that He was God. In Mark 4:37–41, we read that while the disciples were crossing the lake in a boat with Jesus, a storm struck, and their boat began to sink. The disciples panicked and awoke Jesus, who was sleeping through it all. He calmed the storm and in the same breath rebuked them for their unbelief. Verse 41 tells us that after Jesus stilled the storm, they were exceedingly terrified. There is at least one thing more frightening than a fierce storm outside your boat: having to face the holiness of God inside your boat.

In the next chapter of Mark, Jesus met a man possessed by a legion of demons. Jesus sent the demons into a herd of pigs and they went headlong into the lake and drowned. The people of the town came out and pleaded with Him to leave their country, (Mark 5:17). Their reaction to Jesus was not because they were resentful about the loss of the pigs. If that had been the case, they would have demanded compensation. Rather, they were terrified in Jesus' holy presence. They clearly sensed that the One to whom all judgment has been committed had come into their midst, and they were terrified of Him.

In Luke 5, Peter was fishing and could not catch anything. The Lord came along and told him where to let his nets down. Peter obeyed, and his catch was so great that he could not haul it in. When he finally got help from another boat to bring in the catch, there were so many fish that both boats began to sink. It was a demonstration to Peter of Jesus' deity. Peter "fell down at Jesus' feet, saying, 'Go away from me Lord, for I am a sinful man.'", (Luke 5:8). All he could see was his own sinfulness when confronted with the power and presence of our holy God.

We need to cultivate this same attitude, remembering that we not only live our lives before the eyes of a holy God, but that His Holy Spirit dwells within us. Being ever mindful of God's presence is vital if we are going to live worshipful lives that glorify Him.

Questions to Ponder:

1. Throughout the scriptures when people entered God's presence (glory) what was the human response?
2. What do you think should be the human response toward a righteous God?
3. When the divinity of Jesus was revealed, how did the disciples (those who followed the Christ) respond?
4. When the divinity of Jesus was revealed, how did people (those who did not follow the Christ) respond?

5. Did there seem to be any difference between the response of the disciples and those who were not disciples? Why or why not?

Fearing the Wrong Thing

William D. Eisenhower states in his article 'Fearing God" in Christianity Today:

We fear men so much because we fear God so little.

Unfortunately, many of us presume that the world is the ultimate threat and that God's function is to offset it. How different this is from the biblical position that God is far scarier than the world .... When we assume that the world is the ultimate threat, we give it unwarranted power, for in truth, the world's threats are temporary. When we expect God to balance the stress of the world, we reduce him to the world's equal .... As I walk with the Lord, I discover that God poses an ominous threat to my ego, but not to me. He rescues me from my delusions, so he may reveal the truth that sets me free. He casts me down, only to lift me up again. He sits in judgment of my sin, but forgives me, nevertheless. Fear of the Lord is the beginning of wisdom but love from the Lord is its completion.[13]

Whenever we fear anything more than God, we have reduced Him, and minimize His greatness and power. We should fear nothing more than we fear God. The fear of the Lord is the antidote to all other types of fear.

Fearing men and their opinions causes us to cower from our responsibilities before God. Any fear that controls us is sin. Paul in 1 Corinthians 6:12 tells us that we are not to be mastered by anything...this would include fear as much as it includes lust.

We are commanded not to be anxious.

Philippians 4:6 Do not be anxious about anything, but in everything, by prayer and petition, with thanksgiving, present your requests to God. NIV

Fear closes us in, so we lose perspective. It creates a small space. One result of losing perspective is whenever we make decisions based in fear, it will invariably be a wrong decision.

We give power to whatever we fear. It is a terrible thing to give power to a "what if", a fantasy, and a vain imagination, but that is exactly what we do when we fear.

Our fear of the Lord is directly proportional to how much we will trust Him. If we fear Him little, we will trust Him little. The opposite is also true.

Psalms 40:3 He put a new song in my mouth, a hymn of praise to our God. Many will see and fear and put their trust in the Lord. NIV

Psalms 115:11 You who fear him, trust in the Lord — he is their help and shield. NIV

A first glance these two ideas seem contradictory. How is one supposed to trust someone they fear? The fear of the Lord has much to do with how majestic we see Him. If we see Him small, we will have little fear of Him, and we will not trust Him. We must fear God before we can trust Him.

Questions to Ponder:

1. What happens to us if we do not properly fear the Lord?
2. What is the foundation for the wrong type of fear?
3. Why are certain types of 'fears' permissible while others are forbidden?

THIRTEEN

THE PROBLEM OF SIN

In chapters two and three we learned that sin was a major issue for five of the seven churches, with Jesus confronting issues in each church. Sin is the greatest hindrance to being alert and ready for the End Times and the Second Coming. It is important to understand what sin really is.

As humans (even Christians), we do not truly understand the problem of sin. We have never experienced what it is like to live without evil. We have lived with sin for so long historically and personally that we are unable to recognize it and therefore do not fight it. We have a responsibility to diligently fight sin. If not, we begin to tolerate it.

Sin is Aggressive

Sin is not a benign problem, but it is a highly aggressive enemy against us. There is a story in Genesis concerning Cain and Abel, which show us this characteristic.

Genesis 4:7-8 {7} "If you do well, will not your countenance be lifted up? And if you do not do well, sin is crouching at the door; and its desire is for you, but you must master it." NASU

God is explaining to Cain that sin is crouching or lurking at the door of his heart. Cain chose to open the door and allow the sin to attack him. There are two options here. Either sin will rule and reign over him or he can keep the door shut and stay free.

Sin is not passive in its nature, but its desire (yes, sin has a desire) is to rule over you. Therefore, we cannot treat sin passively. We must have the attitude of eradication toward all sin, complete victory must be our mindset. Jesus addresses this issue in the Gospels when He is speaking about the kingdom of God.

Matthew 11:12 "From the days of John the Baptist until now the kingdom of heaven suffers violence, and violent men take it by force. NASU

We Christians must be aggressive towards sin. We are not going to enter God's Kingdom passively but with aggressive determination. Paul tells us what the kingdom of God is.

Romans 14:17 for the kingdom of God is not eating and drinking, but righteousness and peace and joy in the Holy Spirit. NASU

The kingdom of God is righteousness, and sin has no place in it. If we are going to live well in God's kingdom, then we must violently and aggressively destroy sin in our lives.

This is our great dilemma. Sin makes us passive. As we saw in Revelation chapters two and three, sin makes us sleepy and unaware of what is happening in us and around us. It is ironic that sin is aggressive against us, and yet it makes us passive toward sin. Sin is a trickster. Let us treat sin in the same manner that it treats us – aggressively.

Sin is Deceitful

Paul discusses this idea of being deceived by sin.

Romans 7:11 For sin, seizing the opportunity afforded by the commandment, deceived me, and through the commandment put me to death. NIV

Sin, deriving strength from the law and threatening death to the transgressor, deceived me and drew me aside to disobedience, promising me gratification, honor, and independence.[1]

There is again this idea of violently seizing us. Not only is sin aggressive, but it is also violent. Sin does not play fair.

Sin never appears to us as it really is. The man huddled on the cabin floor was slowly freezing to death. It was high in the Rockies in southwestern Alberta, and outside a blizzard raged. John Elliott had logged miles that day through the deep snows of the mountain passes, on high alert for life-threatening avalanches. As dusk settled around him, exhaustion overcame him, and he wearily staggered to his cabin. Dazed with fatigue, he collapsed onto his bed without lighting a fire or removing his wet clothing. As the blizzard blasted through the cracks in the old cabin walls, the sleeping forest ranger sank into oblivion, paralyzed by the pleasure of the storm's icy caress. Suddenly his dog sprang into action and, with unrelenting whines, managed to rouse his near-comatose friend. The dog was John's constant companion, a St. Bernard, one of a long line of dogs famous for their heroics in times of crisis. "If that dog hadn't been with me, I'd be dead today," John Elliott says. "When you're freezing to death you actually feel warm all over, and don't wake up because it feels too good."

This moving story illustrates the spiritual condition of many people today. They are cold spiritually and, sadly, are oblivious of their true condition. Thank God for all the ways in which He arouses such sleepers. He sends His messengers to nudge them awake. Sometimes the methods used to awaken them are drastic, but always for their good. Let us not think that because He shakes us, He therefore hates us. He awakens us from lethargy because He loves us and wants to save us from meaningless life, or worse, an eternal death. When we were "ready to perish" (Isaiah 27:13), He was "ready to save" (Isaiah 38:20). Trust your life in His hand.[2]

What is the mechanism that sin uses to deceive us? It is the pleasure of sin that sin uses to deceive us.

Hebrews 11:25 He chose to be mistreated along with the people of God rather than to enjoy the pleasures of sin for a short time. NIV

In the original language 'the pleasure of sin' has the idea of "full enjoyment". Sin allows and even wants us to take full enjoyment in the sin. By doing so, we are distracted by the actual work that sin is doing in our lives until it is too late.

The enjoyment is only for a short time, for the occasion only, i.e., temporary.

All sin has two faces. In its deceit, sin will only present the beautiful face or side of itself. This is the pleasure side of sin. We must remember that this beautiful side is only an illusion. While we are enjoying the pleasure of the sin yet our unnoticed reality is quite different.

Below the surface an unnoticed dynamic is working – the utter destruction of sin. The reason this dynamic is so effective is because the "pleasure of sin" is the anesthesia to the "pain of sin". The enjoyment of sin acts as a mask to cover the destruction sin is causing. The inability to feel pain is the deadly compromise of what should be an effective defense mechanism (i.e., pain).

The pleasure of sin acts in a similar manner as anesthesia. The person receiving anesthesia falls asleep and feels nothing as the doctor cuts and then sews them back up. It is not until later that the person begins to feel the pain of what happened, but it is too late to prevent the pain. What has happened has happened and now the person is left to figure out how to best cope with the pain that has been left behind.

The desire to rid one's self of pain creates a desire to experience the pleasure of sin again. When we are experiencing the pleasure of sin, we no longer feel the pain of the sin. However, as soon as the season of enjoyment has ended the pain will be even greater. The shame, the guilt, fear, and the misery increase with each experience.

The pain we feel is meant to draw us to the only One who can truly heal us. However instead of moving toward God, we choose to use sin as a temporary method of dealing with our pain. So, we increase our sin, which then increases our shame, fear, and guilt. So, like Adam and Eve, we run away from God and hide, living unnecessarily with destruction and pain.

Sin is Highly Destructive

We know life was perfect before sin. In all of creation there was no pain, suffering, trouble, sickness, death, or any type of relational problems.

Realizing and agreeing with God's perspective about sin's destruction is an issue of faith. Every sin has within its nature the seeds of death and destruction. This means that every time we sin there is death and destruction working in our life. Sometimes this work is imperceivable and other times it is quite obvious.

It is the work of destruction going unnoticed that is the most dangerous. We falsely believe "nothing happened", that we got by with the sin. Because we do not believe what God says about sin, we are easily deceived by sin.

It is the sin of the sinner that keeps him out of heaven.

Romans 6:23 For the wages of sin is death, but the free gift of God is eternal life in Christ Jesus our Lord. NASU

Sin can only produce decay, ruin, and corruption according to Galatians 6:8. No good can ever come out of sin. It is a destruction that comes with corruption.

Galatians 6: 8 For the one who sows to his own flesh will from the flesh reap corruption, but the one who sows to the Spirit will from the Spirit reap eternal life. NASU

James 1:15 Then when lust has conceived, it gives birth to sin; and when sin is accomplished, it brings forth death. 16 Do not be deceived, my beloved brethren. NASU

Rather than living with sin like a good friend, we should understand sin as a mortal enemy, who at every moment desires to kill us. It is crouching, waiting to pounce and destroy.

Sin is the Reason for the Death of Christ

The greatest problem with sin is that it is the reason for the death of Jesus Christ, God's own beloved son. This alone should give us ample motivation for viewing sin as God sees it. Our ugly and wretched sin is the reason Christ hung on the cross. We would do well to stop right now to meditate on this.

We cannot win over sin when we decide to practice sin. Sin is not okay. Sin weakens us, confuses us, and destroys us every time. If that is not enough motivation, God also disciplines us for our sins of which we will not let go. Sin is a no-win proposition.

Sin Must Always be Punished

In the book of Exodus, we read the of the nature and character of God. It is God's revelation of Himself to us and this is what He says about Himself.

Exodus 34:5-7 {5} The Lord descended in the cloud and stood there with him as he called upon the name of the Lord. 6 Then the Lord passed by in front of him and proclaimed, "The Lord, the Lord God, compassionate and gracious, slow to anger, and abounding in lovingkindness and truth; 7 who keeps lovingkindness for thousands, who forgives iniquity, transgression and sin; yet He will by no means leave the guilty unpunished, visiting the iniquity of fathers on the children and on the grandchildren to the third and fourth generations." NASU

There is no question about God's goodness, kindness, compassion, and graciousness. However, there is another side to God that cannot be ignored. It is His justice side...He must punish sin and He does so every time. Within sin's nature are the consequences of sin – destruction and death.

Sin is a veritable cyanide pill. It may be a quick-acting pill or a slow-release capsule, but the end result is the same – death.

It is true that in Christ we have escaped eternal punishment, but we do not escape the consequences of our sins here on earth. We must choose not to sin.

Questions to Ponder:

1. What is my attitude about sin?
2. What is God's attitude toward sin? Are my attitude and God's attitude in agreement?
3. Do I genuinely believe that God punishes sin?

Being Intolerant of Any and All Sin

Preparing for the End Times and the Second Coming requires us to have a "zero tolerance" attitude toward sin. Anything less than this type of thinking will leave us in a vulnerable position that could have negative and even eternal consequences.

If sin is chosen today, when life is easy why would we choose Jesus when the stakes are high? That is delusional thinking. The rule of thumb is this, "What we do today is what we will do tomorrow."

We are too good at denial, blameshifting, ignoring, believing it is okay, and making excuses for our sins. However, this thinking does not diminish or eliminate the effects of sin in our life or God's discipline.

We need to be firmly rooted and grounded in the Word. If we are choosing to sin, then we cannot be rooted properly. The result will be a lack of the strength to remain strong and steadfast in the times of trouble.

King David is an example of this. Before his sin with Bathsheba, King David was a powerful king and an exceptional general. God said he was a man after His own heart. However, after sleeping with Bathsheba and having her husband killed, he no longer carried the power as before. He did not discipline the sexual immorality within his family, made a sinful decision numbering the people, and he inappropriately mourned over the death of his usurping son. The consequences of David's sin have continued in his household until today, (2 Samuel 12:10-22).

Sin cripples us, putting us at an extreme disadvantage. We are unable to love properly causing our hearts to grow cold. This coldness will not allow us to endure to the end.

Matthew 24:12-13 {12} "Because lawlessness is increased, most people's love will grow cold. 13 "But the one who endures to the end, he will be saved. NASU

Questions to Ponder:

1. Am I tolerating sin in my life? If so, why?
2. In what ways do I see the sins in my life causing weakness?

The Problem of Compromise

There is a right and proper use of the word compromise. However, in this description of the word, we are looking at the wrong use of the word compromise. This lesson is dealing with inappropriate and sinful compromise. The idea of "compromising" is man's idea, not God's. God does not compromise with sin. Compromise is an effort to make us feel better about our sin (at least I sort of obeyed). Whenever we take an idea contrary to God's word and apply it to our situation we have compromised (sinned). In God's view there are not degrees of compromise; He just sees sin. We think of compromise as partial or mostly obedience, but partial obedience is disobedience.

A little compromise of righteousness is unrighteous. Trying to minimize your sin by adding a few righteous acts on it does not change the fact that it is sin.

Compromise is rooted in excuses, justifications, exceptions, and reasons as to why complete obedience is not necessary. Compromise allows us to wrongly think that our situation is special, unique, or too difficult. We convince ourselves God would not demand the impossible and therefore lesser obedience is acceptable. There is an excellent story in the Old Testament that helps us understand this idea.

In 1 Samuel 15 Samuel commands Saul to go and destroy all the Amalekites and everything they owned because of what they previously did to Israel when they were coming out of Egypt. Saul dutifully goes out to perform the charge. It says that he did what he was commanded to do, but verse nine speaks of a compromise.

1 Samuel 15:9 But Saul and the people spared Agag and the best of the sheep, the oxen, the fatlings, the lambs, and all that was good, and were not willing to destroy them utterly; but everything despised and worthless, that they utterly destroyed. NASU

As a result, the Lord tells Samuel he regrets making Saul king. So, the Lord sends Samuel to confront the compromise of Saul.

1 Samuel 15:19-22 {19} "Why then did you not obey the voice of the Lord, but rushed upon the spoil and did what was evil in the sight of the Lord?"

20 Then Saul said to Samuel, "I did obey the voice of the Lord, and went on the mission on which the Lord sent me, and have brought back Agag the king of Amalek, and have utterly destroyed the Amalekites. 21 "But the people took some of the spoil, sheep and oxen, the choicest of the things devoted to destruction, to sacrifice to the Lord your God at Gilgal." NASU

We see Saul justifying his actions, saying that he did obey, and blameshifting onto the people his disobedience. For this disobedience Saul loses his kingship. This is what we call compromise – partial obedience. Partial obedience / compromise is not obedience, but it is sin.

A key characteristic of compromise is pride. Pride is blinding, so we are easily convinced our compromised perceptions are correct. In the end, we carelessly blend our sinful ideas with God's word. This has deadly results.

1 Samuel 15:17 Samuel said, "Is it not true, though you were little in your own eyes, you were made the head of the tribes of Israel? And the Lord anointed you king over Israel, NASU

It was because of Saul's pride he thought he did not have to completely obey. His reasonings were correct and acceptable in his own sight.

One of Aesop's fables bring this point home quite well is the "The Farmer and the Snake".

A farmer walked through his field one cold winter morning. On the ground lay a snake, stiff and frozen with the cold. The farmer knew how deadly the snake could be, and yet he picked it up and put it in his bosom to warm it back to life.

The snake soon revived, and when it had enough strength, bit the man who had been so kind to it. The bite was deadly, and the farmer felt that he must die. As he drew his last breath, he said to those standing around: "Learn from my fate, do not to take pity on a scoundrel."

The farmer in his arrogance believed that if he were kind to the snake, then the snake would appreciate the kindness, even though the farmer knew the snake to be deadly. In this story the farmer compromised what he knew was good sense and what was right (leave the snake alone). Sin always bites and its venom is always deadly.

Compromise is the opposite of absolutes. Truth never changes; it cannot change as it is solidly entrenched in righteousness. However, compromise constantly requires change.

Compromise is insatiable and demands more compromise. People wrongly believe if they give just a little, then compromise will be satisfied. This is never the case. The giving up of truth to compromise ends in the death of truth.

Compromise is embedded in fear and a lack of trust in God. It is the fear of loss and pain. We fear the loss of future opportunity, loss of acceptance, loss of the material possessions, or the loss reputation. We do not believe that God will take proper care of us and that His grace will be insufficient. He may even invite us into suffering.

We need to stand strong in the face of unrighteousness and be fully determined to obey in every situation.

Questions to Ponder:

1. In what ways and in what areas have I been compromising?
2. Why is morally compromising so dangerous?
3. Why do I find myself compromising in areas where I should not be compromising?

Killing Evil Desires

Many people believe evil desires are not sinful. They say you can desire something and it is okay but you cannot act on that desire or it is sin. However, is this what the Bible really says or is this wishful thinking?

What does the Bible say about evil desires? Can we allow them to lie dormant?

Colossians 3:5 Put to death, therefore, whatever belongs to your earthly nature: sexual immorality, impurity, lust, evil desires, and greed, which is idolatry. NIV

2 Peter 2:10 This is especially true of those who follow the corrupt desire of the sinful nature and despise authority. NIV

Ephesians 4:22 that, in reference to your former manner of life, you lay aside the old self, which is being corrupted in accordance with the lusts of deceit. NASU

Matthew 5:28 but I say to you that everyone who looks at a woman with lust for her has already committed adultery with her in his heart. NASU

James 1:13-15 {14} But each one is tempted when he is carried away and enticed by his own lust. 15 Then when lust has conceived, it gives birth to sin; and when sin is accomplished, it brings forth death. NASU

From these scriptures mentioned above, we know sinful desires are never okay to have. These verses tell us clearly evil desires are a horrific problem. Our focus should be to destroy them, as this is where the root of the problem lies.

When a genuine believer sins it is because he or she wants to sin.

Paul in the book of Colossians tells us to put to death evil desires. If evil desires are so benign, then why would this action be necessary? Evil desires are highly toxic and dangerous.

Paul, and Peter both write evil desires are corrupting. They destroy the inner man. We cannot allow them to remain. These evil desires cause us to spiritually shrivel until we are destroyed.

James then tells us that the only reason we are tempted to sin is because of the evil desires we have. These evil desires draw us away and entice us to sin. Logically then, if we destroy our evil desires, then we take away our temptation to sin.

Jesus in the book of Matthew explains just lusting (having evil sensual desires) toward a woman is committing adultery in one's heart. Jesus informs us evil desires are sin.

If we are trying to stop sinful actions and allow sinful desires to remain, then we have put ourselves in an impossible situation. By putting to death evil desires, we will stop sinful actions. We must not harbor lustful and evil desires in our hearts.

Another point to remember is as believers we are no longer a slave to sin. We have been given the power to overcome all sin. Peter reminds us what God has given us. We have the divine power, the Holy Spirit living in us and now we are free from the power of sin.

2 Peter 1:3 seeing that His divine power has granted to us everything pertaining to life and godliness, through the true knowledge of Him who called us by His own glory and excellence... NASU

We have been made free. Now, we have a choice not to sin. So, when a genuine believer sins it is because he or she wants to sin. We are choosing to sin.

Questions to Ponder:

1. Have I been dealing with my evil desires according to the Scriptures? If not, what needs to change? How will I make these changes?
2. How is my struggle to overcome specific sins linked to my evil desires?

FOURTEEN

ETERNAL PUNISHMENT

Jesus talks about hell more than he talks about heaven and describes it more vividly. There is no denying that Jesus knew, believed, and warned against the absolute reality of hell.

No book on the Second Coming would be complete without a section on eternal punishment. This chapter is not meant to be a comprehensive study, but to show the biblical reality of eternal punishment.

There are unfortunately two popular views on hell that are present in recent church culture: (1) There is no literal hell and (2) there is no eternal judgement. The latter of the two positions believes in a hell and judgement that moves towards annihilation rather than eternal punishment.

Those who have morphed the true God of the Bible into a false god of their minds greatly struggle with the idea of God punishing people in hell for eternity. They are unwilling and unable to reconcile who they think God is with the reality of hell. God tells us who He is, but we finite beings cannot comprehend the infinite God so we try to redefine Him into our image. Great care needs to be given that we do not humanize God.

When trying to understand the Bible, it is important to start our study with clear and plain scriptures. Then we can work toward the more obscure verses. No one should ever use an obscure passage to interpret obvious and easy to understand scriptures.

What did Jesus say about hell?

It is ironic that people use only one characteristic of Jesus (love) to minimize the severity or to dismiss the idea of hell altogether. This is interesting because Jesus talked about hell more than any other person in the Bible, and He discusses it in detail more than He does heaven. So, why would a loving Jesus talk about such a horrible place more than any other person in the Bible? Does Jesus know something that we struggle with and desire to deny?

Jesus is the truth and always speaks the truth. We know that Jesus would not say something or convey an idea that was not truthful. It is extremely important that we take Jesus at His words. It would be wrong to reformat, reinvent, change, or construe them into something else. There were plenty of ways and words available to Jesus to convey a different idea of "hell" if He was truly wanting to say something different. It is for this reason we must understand hell as a real place.

Hell is a real place

We begin with the Sermon on the Mount, which is the first sermon Jesus preached. It was at this time He introduced the spiritual kingdom of God, which included a warning about hell. Why in His first sermon would He bring up the topic of hell? The Jews at this time clearly understood 'Gehenna' (the word for hell) as a literal place of punishment for the wicked dead.[1]

This approach is certainly counterintuitive to our human thinking. Talking about such a negative subject was not the way to begin His ministry. Who would want to listen to this type of teaching? Why not just leave the topic out? Jesus knew that it was important for people to know the whole truth. He is telling the crowd, "Here is the kingdom of God and here is the alternative if you choose not to live in my kingdom.

Matthew 5:22 "But I say to you that everyone who is angry with his brother shall be guilty before the court; and whoever says to his brother, 'You good-for-nothing,' shall be guilty before the supreme court; and whoever says, 'You fool,' shall be guilty enough **to go into the fiery hell**. NASU

Jesus gives us the first description of hell. It is a place to go into and it is fiery. The wording expresses both a physical location and fire as a physical element. This leads to the natural conclusion that hell is a literal place to go to and there is pain and suffering in it. The lack of explanation about hell implies the audience had a basic understanding of what Jesus was saying about it.

Matthew 5:29-30 {29} "If your right eye makes you stumble, tear it out and throw it from you; for it is better for you to lose one of the parts of your body, than for your **whole body to be thrown into hell**. 30 "If your right hand makes you stumble, cut it off and throw it from you; for it is better for you to lose one of the parts of your body, than for your **whole body to go into hell**. NASU

Again, we see the literal aspect of hell. Jesus speaks of the whole physical body being thrown into hell. One does not throw a physical body into an idea or into an allegory. The original language describes it as a violent or intense throwing rather than a casual toss. We know from other scriptures that it is God who is doing the throwing.

Matthew 10:28 "Do not fear those who kill the body but are unable to kill the soul; but rather fear Him who is able to destroy both soul and body in hell. NASU

The word destroy is to do it completely, in its entirety; to put an end to, ruin. It is absolute destruction. In the Old Testament this word is used one hundred and eighty-four times. The meaning of this word is not our modern idea of annihilation (ceasing to exist eternally, oblivion).

In the New Testament the word is used eighty-nine times and means to destroy fully, perish, or lose. It is never translated annihilation.

Jesus is teaching about having an eternal perspective because there is an eternal consequence. Those in hell will suffer the complete destruction of their bodies and souls.

Matthew 23:15 "Woe to you, scribes and Pharisees, hypocrites, because you travel around on sea and land to make one proselyte; and when he becomes one, you make him twice as much a son of hell as yourselves. NASU

Matthew 23:33 "You serpents, you brood of vipers, how will you escape the sentence of hell? NASU

Here again we see Jesus referencing hell and speaking about it as a literal place of judgement. People do not choose hell. They are sentenced to hell by God, as it is a punishment.[2] He is making it clear that this was something that the Pharisees were going to experience.

Luke 10:15 "And you, Capernaum, will not be exalted to heaven, will you? You will be brought down to Hades! NASU

In the Bible there are two other words describing hell: Sheol and Hades. Sheol is the Old Testament word (first mentioned in Deuteronomy 32:22) and Hades is the New Testament equivalent. Both these words refer to the underworld of fiery hell. In this passage and the verses previous, Jesus is pronouncing judgement on different cities that have rejected Him and His message.

Luke 16:23 "In Hades he lifted up his eyes, being in torment, and saw Abraham far away and Lazarus in his bosom. NASU

This is a story Jesus is telling about the rich man and Lazarus. The rich man is in Hades and he is suffering and being tormented. The punishment he is enduring is real and personal. He speaks of fire, heat, and thirst as part of his agony. He realizes that this is not a place from which he can escape and begs Lazarus to bring him water and to go warn his brothers. (Note: it is quite interesting that the rich man did not ask to be set free from Hades. It is as if he intuitively understood that this was his punishment for rejecting God and his ways.)

Jesus is not telling a fairytale to scare us. He is telling us the truth to warn us.

Matthew 25:46 "These will go away into eternal punishment, but the righteous into eternal life." NASU

In Matthew 25:46 Jesus has just separated His true disciples from those that rejected Him. He says that the goats are going away to eternal punishment, but the righteous to eternal life. There are a couple of important observations to make. First, there is a personal punishment that is eternal. The word eternal means forever, without end. For a punishment to be a punishment there must be consciousness or awareness of suffering and pain, which the original word suggests.

For example, if someone says they are going to punish a dead body by beating it, is it a punishment for the dead body? No, the body has no consciousness or awareness, so there is no sense of punishment.

Second, if we eliminate the idea of everlasting punishment, we must also eliminate the idea of everlasting life. It is the same word for both. We want the one without the other. This is not possible. The human soul is eternal without end.

Hell is a place of judgement

This is an important point as well as difficult. It is hard to understand a loving God sending people to a place of eternal torment. This is because we fail to understand both the severity of sin and the justice of God in its fulness. We cannot eliminate or minimize one attribute of God at the expense of another. All His attributes must be equally true, as this is what makes Him God. He does not need to fit into our human mold of limited understanding.

Matthew 13:36-43 {36} Then He left the crowds and went into the house. And His disciples came to Him and said, "Explain to us the parable of the tares of the field." 37 And He said, "The one who sows the good seed is the Son of Man, 38 and the field is the world; and as for the good seed, these are the sons of the kingdom; and the tares are the sons of the evil one; 39 and the enemy who sowed them is the devil, and the harvest is the end of the age; and the reapers are angels. 40 "So just as the tares are gathered up and burned with fire, so shall it be at the end of the age. 41 "The Son of Man will send forth His angels, and they will gather out of His kingdom all stumbling blocks, and those who commit lawlessness, 42 and will throw them into the furnace of fire; in that place there will be weeping and gnashing of teeth. 43 "Then THE RIGHTEOUS WILL SHINE FORTH AS THE SUN in the kingdom of their Father. He who has ears, let him hear. NASU

The setting for Matthew 13 is confused disciples trying to understand the parables of the tares that He had just told to the crowds. The disciples gathered around Him afterwards and asked Him to explain what He had just said. It is here that Jesus who knows what hell is (as He originally created it for the angels) explaining its frightful characteristics.

- It is a place where people are burned with fire. In hell people will feel the pain of heat and fire.
- It is a furnace of fire. Hell is a place of intense fire and heat.
- It is a place of weeping. This is a place of great sorrow, despair, and sadness (emotional pain).
- It is a place of gnashing teeth. Here there is also physical pain as well as anger, resentment, and unrepentance. The idea of gnashing is that of rage and fury.

Matthew 13:47-50 {47} "Again, the kingdom of heaven is like a dragnet cast into the sea, and gathering fish of every kind; 48 and when it was filled, they drew it up on the beach; and they sat down and gathered the good fish into containers, but the bad they threw away. 49 "So it will be at the end of the age; the angels will come forth and take out the wicked from among the righteous, 50 and will throw them into the furnace of fire; in that place there will be weeping and gnashing of teeth. NASU

We should not miss the significance of Jesus repeating the same words. This repetition confirms the veracity of what He is saying. We cannot miss the point.

There was a church member who was tired of the sermons on hell and told the pastor to preach about the 'meek and lowly' Jesus; to which the pastor replied that is where I got my information on hell.

Matthew 22:11-13 {11} "But when the king came in to look over the dinner guests, he saw a man there who was not dressed in wedding clothes, 12 and he said to him, 'Friend, how did you come in here without wedding clothes?' And the man was speechless. 13 "Then the king said to the servants, 'Bind him hand and foot, and throw him into the outer darkness; in that place there will be weeping and gnashing of teeth.' NASU

Jesus gives more description as to what hell is like. He adds the phrase 'bind him hand and foot'. There is no resistance strong enough to withstand the Sovereign Lord. This idea tells us no one of their own volition is choosing hell.

In earlier descriptions hell was a furnace of fire, but here Jesus chooses the phrase outer darkness. The wicked while they are alive graciously live under the light of God, but the day will come when for them there will be no presence of God...it will be outer darkness. This is a place where there is no hope for a different outcome. It is where the darkness is so dark that it can be felt.

Matthew 24:50-51 {50} the master of that slave will come on a day when he does not expect him and at an hour which he does not know, 51 and will cut him in pieces and assign him a place with the hypocrites; in that place there will be weeping and gnashing of teeth. NASU

Again, we find similarity, but also added new details. The phrase 'will cut him pieces' is extreme. The punishment of the wicked will be extreme. We must remember Jesus is doing the talking, He is telling the story. Jesus could have said something far less offensive and extreme, but He did not. What He wants is for us to take what He is saying to heart and seriously. Hell is not a place anyone would choose to be. It is a severe punishment.

Matthew 25:29-30 {29} "For to everyone who has, more shall be given, and he will have an abundance; but from the one who does not have, even what he does have shall be taken away. 30 "Throw out the worthless slave into the outer darkness; in that place there will be weeping and gnashing of teeth. NASU

Matthew 25:41 "Then He will also say to those on His left, 'Depart from Me, accursed ones, into the eternal fire which has been prepared for the devil and his angels; NASU

Jesus repeats himself again, reiterating the truth of hell. He says that it is an eternal fire that was prepared for the devil and his angels. Those who choose the lies of Satan will suffer eternally with Satan.

Mark 9:42-48 {42} "Whoever causes one of these little ones who believe to stumble, it would be better for him if, with a heavy millstone hung around his neck, he had been cast into the sea. 43 "If your hand causes you to stumble, cut it off; it is better for you to enter life crippled, than, having your two hands, to go into hell, into the unquenchable fire, 44 [where THEIR WORM DOES NOT DIE, AND THE FIRE IS NOT QUENCHED.] 45 "If your foot causes you to stumble, cut it off; it is better for you to enter life lame, than, having your two feet, to be cast into hell, 46 [where THEIR

WORM DOES NOT DIE, AND THE FIRE IS NOT QUENCHED.]
47 "If your eye causes you to stumble, throw it out; it is better for you to
enter the kingdom of God with one eye, than, having two eyes, to be cast
into hell, 48 where THEIR WORM DOES NOT DIE, AND THE FIRE
IS NOT QUENCHED. NASU

Jesus is using a unique phrase here to describe the judgement / punishment
of hell. It is speaking of an internal torment and an external torment. The
main idea is that it is an eternal torment.

Hell is forever

We have discussed this idea in the earlier sections above.

Hell is more terrible than we can imagine

Jesus has given us sufficient information for us to know that hell is not a
fairytale that He contrived. Hell is a reality so terrible we can hardly
conceive it. It was not intended for humans, but for the rebelling devil and
his angels. He wants us to know of its horrible reality.

New Testament Writers

We have reviewed what Jesus said about hell. Now let us consider what
other New Testament writers wrote about hell. It is interesting that the
word 'hell' itself only appears two times outside of the Gospels (James and
2 Peter). The New Testament writers spoke a great deal about the Second
Coming, but they used other words or ideas to express the reality of hell.

Paul

Philippians 3:19 (whose end is destruction)

1 Thessalonians 1:9 (eternal destruction)

John

Revelation 14:9 (the wine of God's wrath and tormented with fire and brimstone)

Revelation 14:10-11 (tormented with fire and brimstone and the smoke of their torment goes up forever and ever)

Revelation 19:20 (the beast and false prophet were thrown alive into the lake of fire)

Revelation 20:10, 13-15 (the devil is thrown into the lake of fire; death and Hades are thrown into the lake of fire, anyone whose name in not written in the book of life is thrown into the lake of fire)

Jude

Jude 1:6 (angels in eternal bonds under darkness)

Jude 1:13 (the eternal black darkness)

James

James 3:6 (the evilness of the tongue has its roots in hell)

Peter

2 Peter 2:4 (angels are cast into hell, the pits of darkness reserved for judgement)

This issue of an eternal hell is so horrible that God in His mercy sends an angel in the Last of the Last days to mankind. The angel gives a verbal warning as he flies in the skies. The warning is "do not worship the beast or receive his mark for in doing so you will receive eternal punishment", (Revelation 14:10-11). God does not want any human to end up in hell.

Whether we like or understand it, the idea of eternal punishment / judge-ment is in the Bible. Jesus by far is the one who spoke about hell the most. Then the apostle who is sometimes referred to as the "Love Apostle", John spoke about hell the second most. Those who love the most speak the most about hell.

This topic is found throughout the Old Testament. A most famous passage in found in Daniel. Everyone arises from the dead. There are those who rise to everlasting life and others to disgrace and everlasting contempt.

Daniel 12:1-3 {1} "Now at that time Michael, the great prince who stands guard over the sons of your people, will arise. And there will be a time of distress such as never occurred since there was a nation until that time; and at that time your people, everyone who is found written in the book, will be rescued. 2 "Many of those who sleep in the dust of the ground will awake, these to everlasting life, but the others to disgrace and everlasting contempt. 3 "Those who have insight will shine brightly like the brightness of the expanse of heaven, and those who lead the many to righteousness, like the stars forever and ever. NASU

It is not God's desire to send people to hell. He takes no pleasure in such a tragedy. But God is a just God, and a rejection of Him has dire and eternal consequences.

Questions to Ponder:

1. How does our idea about hell and eternal judgement need to change?
2. How should we increase our awareness of this idea of eternal judgement?
3. In what ways would or should the concept of eternal judgement affect our choices and lifestyle?

FIFTEEN

THE CONCLUSION

There are many things that could help us prepare for the Second Coming, but the ideas that were chosen for the chapters in this book came from Revelation chapters one, two, and three. These are the things Jesus emphasizes in these scriptures, so we expounded and expanded them.

You might have expected a book with specific details about the End Times and the Second Coming, but this book intentionally focuses on our spiritual personal preparation for those times. It is my hope this book has challenged you to think about the End Times and the Second Coming and how to better prepare for them. But thinking about these times and how to prepare is meaningless unless you actually take action and begin to prepare. It would be a horrible shame to have read this book and think, "Wow, that was challenging!" and then do nothing. Please do not allow that to happen.

Jesus is coming back so we must prepare

Jesus is coming back; this we know for sure. So, it is important that we make ourselves alert and ready. The preparation Jesus was discussing in Revelation did not consider the material aspects. The reason is because this is of far lesser importance than being spiritually and mentally prepared. It does not mean that we should not prepare in the materialistic sense, but this was not an emphasis of Jesus. If we are materially prepared for the End Times, but not spiritually prepared, we will fail.

If we fear God properly, then we will fear nothing else. This means if we are fearing the future, we need to fear God more. For the believer, the events to come will be a trial like nothing anyone has ever gone through since time began. Therefore, proper preparation is necessary so that we can truly enjoy the Second Coming of Christ as the most glorious event of all time. This will only be true if we have properly prepared by making ourselves alert and ready.

It is self-defeating to choose to remain ignorant, pretending, or denying that these times before the Second Coming will not be difficult. They will be filled with tremendous trouble that has never been seen before. There are Christians who believe that tribulation is something we will not have to endure, because we have a way out before the great trouble begins. However, what if that is not a correct understanding? What if we are meant to endure the suffering in these last days as Christians have all throughout time? Would it be wiser to properly prepare spiritually for these difficult times than to hope we do not go through them? If we are removed before all the suffering begins, then we will certainly be more like Christ than if we had done nothing to prepare. We should plan as if we are going to be in the thick of trouble rather than hoping we will not be.

There is an important question for us to consider: How are we currently doing spiritually, mentally, and emotionally with our current trouble and difficulty? If we are filled with dread, fear, worry, or anxiety, then this is a clue and warning that we are not properly prepared for what is to come. This is a difficult and uncomfortable conclusion. There is no such thing in the Bible as 'noble fear' or 'justified worry' or 'reasonable anxiousness'. These things are all sin and shows a lack of trust in the Lord, which is also a sin. These wrong negative emotions betray our faith in the Lord. Neither fear or unbelief allow faith to work as we see in the story below.

Mark 5:38-43 {38} They came to the house of the synagogue official; and He saw a commotion, and people loudly weeping and wailing. 39 And entering in, He said to them, "Why make a commotion and weep? The child has not died, but is asleep." 40 They began laughing at Him. But putting them all out, He took along the child's father and mother and His own companions, and entered the room where the child was. 41 Taking the child by the hand, He said to her, "Talitha kum!" (which translated means, "Little girl, I say to you, get up!"). 42 Immediately the girl got up and began to walk, for she was twelve years old. And immediately they were completely astounded. NASU

Because of their unbelief Jesus sent the people out of the house. Unbelief and faith cannot exist in the same house. As long as there is unbelief, Jesus could not perform the miracle.

In these last days there will be a great falling away. For sure, most of those who fall away will be the pretenders and the fakes. However, there will also be those who are genuine, but who were not prepared for this time. These will not have the strength to endure.

How then should we live? What is Jesus requiring of us? We must live in a manner that honors and glorifies the Lord. It is necessary to have an all-in heart that is willing to lose everything for Christ, that is willing to die for Christ. For us to know with confidence that we are willing to lose everything and die for Jesus, we must currently be living a life of self-denial and daily taking up our cross. If this is how we are living now, then we can rest assured we will do it in the future.

If we were expecting a visit from our favorite grandparents for Christmas, we would be thinking about it often before they arrived. We would have great anticipation and excitement every time we would think about their visit. Oh, the joy! Also, we would prepare for their coming by making sure everything was in order and right. The house would be cleaned and their room beautifully decorated. We might even fix them special foods in advance. We would leave nothing to chance.

So, what about us today? The culmination of time, the greatest event, that will ever take place, is right before us; so, let us not overlook it. If our thoughts are distracted and unfocused, then we are thinking of our needs for tomorrow without thought to our eternity. Truly, we must reprioritize our values and set our affections on the things above. So many today live as if the Second Coming is never going to happen.

One reason we are lackadaisical about the Second Coming is that people have made predictions and have been wrong. Repeatedly we have been disillusioned and disappointed. None of us want to be disappointed again, so it is easier just to not think about it.

There is a story that brings this point home. It is "The Boy Who Cried Wolf". In this story there was a shepherd boy who would cry wolf when there was no wolf. The villagers would come running only to find out that he was tricking them. Eventually, the villagers decided not to respond to the next time the shepherd boy yelled out, "Wolf". Sure enough, the boy did it again, but the villagers were unresponsive. Unfortunately, this time when the boy yelled out wolf, there was really a wolf. The wolf ravaged and killed the sheep. The villagers had become weary of hearing the cry, "Wolf" when there was no wolf.

We do hear a great deal about Jesus coming back, but we do not want to become like the villagers who became unresponsive and disinterested. Even though it has been a long time humanly speaking, and we have heard the message so many times, we must still not grow weary in well doing. We should continuously work diligently to be responsive and remain alert and ready.

Allowing ourselves to grow complacent about the Second Coming is something we can never do. This is exactly what Jesus warned we should not do.

Live with an eternal perspective

Whether Jesus comes tomorrow or in ten years or even longer is not the point. We should be living our life as if He were coming tomorrow. This is a difficult task for us to do. For many of us, it requires a completely new set of values and priorities along with a totally different way of living. If we do not make this change, then we will be creating a more difficult future for ourselves. We can pay the price now or later, but we all must pay the price. However, the price later is always more expensive than now.

There are only two choices for us. Either we are daily and diligently preparing for the End Times and Second Coming, or we are growing careless, neglectful, and adopting poor values and priorities. There is no in-between. There are no other alternatives. So, if we are not preparing, then by default we are growing careless and neglectful. Certainly, this is a sober thought, but nonetheless it is the truth.

If it is too difficult to imagine a future time of Christ's return, then perhaps our own death can become the motivation for changing our lives, so we can be alert and ready. This idea is closer to home for many of us and may seem more relatable. We should have the same preparation theology for meeting Jesus at our death as we would at His Second Coming. The preparation for both events would be the same. We must think eternally. Both ideas should cause us to think how we are building and with what are we building.

Paul in 1 Corinthians three speaks to us about this idea.

1 Corinthians 3:12-15 {12} Now if any man builds on the foundation with gold, silver, precious stones, wood, hay, straw, 13 each man's work will become evident; for the day will show it because it is to be revealed with fire, and the fire itself will test the quality of each man's work. 14 If any man's work which he has built on it remains, he will receive a reward. 15 If any man's work is burned up, he will suffer loss; but he himself will be saved, yet so as through fire. NASU

We must have an eternal perspective or we will use the wrong materials, in which, our works are burned up. What is wood, hay and straw? How do we know if we are building with them? What is the fire? These are important questions to find the answers to. We do not want to be disappointed in the end.

Build your life with the right materials

Isaiah gives us an idea as to what Paul was alluding to here in the Old Testament.

Isaiah 5:24-25 {24} Therefore, as a tongue of fire consumes stubble and dry grass collapses into the flame, so their root will become like rot and their blossom blow away as dust; For they have rejected the law of the Lord of hosts and despised the word of the Holy One of Israel. 25 On this account the anger of the Lord has burned against His people, and He has stretched out His hand against them and struck them down. and the mountains quaked, and their corpses lay like refuse in the middle of the streets. For all this His anger is not spent, but His hand is still stretched out. NASU

The bottom line is the rejection of the law of the Lord and a despising of the word of the Holy One. No genuine Christian would ever think of outrightly rejecting and despising the word of the Lord. However, how we approach, choose to understand, and practice the word of God is what determines we are rejecting and despising God's word.

There are a couple of examples that will show us if we are building with wood, hay, or stubble. Everything centers on the word of God and what we are thinking and believing about the word of God.

- The Prosperity Gospel, which is a false gospel and really is no gospel at all. This teaching encourages materialism, greed, and covetousness. If you want something for yourself, then just speak it into reality. Use your faith not to draw closer to God, but to gain more stuff. This is building a life with wood, hay, and straw.

- God is love and there is no judgement in Him at all. This is also a false idea. (Hopefully, in this book you have read some of the hard things that loving Jesus said to His churches.) This teaching goes soft on sin and confronting sin. There is the prevailing attitude about sin, "No worries; God forgives all your sins." While this is true if you are in Christ, there is also an equally true other idea. God always punishes every sin, even though He forgives you. To only believe one side of the equation and live accordingly is to build with wood, hay, and straw.

Psalms 119:7-11 speaks of the right attitude necessary for receiving the laws of God. We all have a great responsibility and that is to believe all the words of Jesus. Just before Jesus returned to heaven, He told His disciples to make disciples teaching them to obey all things I have commanded. Whenever we decide to select what we are going to listen to and obey, we are building with wood, hay, and straw.

Verse 14 makes an interesting statement. Paul says, "If any man's work which he has built on it remains..." What is the work that Paul is talking about?

What is our work?

Jesus explains what our work is.

John 6:29 Jesus answered and said to them, "This is the work of God, that you believe in Him whom He has sent." NASU

John 5:37-38 {37} "And the Father who sent Me, He has testified of Me. You have neither heard His voice at any time nor seen His form. 38 "You do not have His word abiding in you, for you do not believe Him whom He sent. NASU

Our work is not only to believe in Jesus, but to believe what He is saying. How do we know if we are believing in Jesus? We obey what He says. If we do not obey all that He says, then we do not believe Him nor do we believe in Him. Our faith and obedience are the only things that will survive the fire.

It is a shame if all that we have strived for and built in this life does not transfer over into the next life. Yes, we make it into eternity with God, but there is nothing to show for at the Judgement Seat of Christ. We want a life that is fixed on the eternal rather than the temporal material world.

What is it that can convince us to honestly consider our values, priorities, choices, and actions, if death or the Second Coming does not move us to reconsider?

Questions to Ponder?

1. What place does the kingdom of God play in our lives? How or what are we doing right now to extend the kingdom of God?
2. Are we currently living in a God fearing and God honoring manner? Will Jesus be able to say, "Well done good and faithful servant"?
3. Are all our relationships in order?
4. What areas of our lives have we identified needing repentance and change?
5. Have we grown careless and complacent in our thinking about the End Times and the Second Coming? If so, how and in what areas?

NOTES

1. Introduction

1. *New American Standard Bible: 1995 update.* (1995). (Mt 24:14). La Habra, CA: The Lockman Foundation.

3. Alert and Ready: Lessons from Ephesus

1. Barton, B., Comfort, P., Osborne, G., Taylor, L. K., & Veerman, D. (2001). *Life Application New Testament Commentary* (p. 1210). Wheaton, IL: Tyndale.

4. Alert and Ready: Lessons from Smyrna

1. Barton, B., Comfort, P., Osborne, G., Taylor, L. K., & Veerman, D. (2001). *Life Application New Testament Commentary* (p. 1211). Wheaton, IL: Tyndale.

5. Alert and Ready: Lessons from Pergamum

1. Barton, B., Comfort, P., Osborne, G., Taylor, L. K., & Veerman, D. (2001). *Life Application New Testament Commentary* (p. 1212). Wheaton, IL: Tyndale.

6. Alert and Ready: Lesson from Thyatira

1. There is only one time when forgiveness removes punishment and that is when we are born again. God at this time removes our eternal punishment. On all other occasions there is always punishment for sin even though God forgives us. Paul tells the Galatians not to be deceived, in that, whatever they sow they will reap. Within sin are the seeds of destruction and death meaning that sin always punishes. There are no exceptions to this law of God.

7. Alert and Ready: Lessons from Sardis

1. Barton, B., Comfort, P., Osborne, G., Taylor, L. K., & Veerman, D. (2001). *Life Application New Testament Commentary* (pp. 1215–1216). Wheaton, IL: Tyndale.

2. Paul, in Romans 1:18-32, speaks of idolatry and sexual immorality as bookend sins. We see in this passage that idolatry given enough time always leads to sexual immorality. Jesus, more than once, connects these two sins together in His letter to the seven churches as well. The idea here is that by speaking of idolatry and sexual immorality there is the of inclusion of all sins.

8. Alert and Ready: Lessons from Philadelphia

1. Barton, B., Comfort, P., Osborne, G., Taylor, L. K., & Veerman, D. (2001). *Life Application New Testament Commentary* (p. 1217). Wheaton, IL: Tyndale.
2. Assuredly, the New Testament writer Paul, who was a natural born Jew, clearly says that in the last days God will again pour out His Spirit on the natural Jews (Israel), in the hopes they will repent and come to Christ.
3. Barton, B. B. (2000). *Revelation.* (G. R. Osborne, Ed.) (p. 44). Wheaton, IL: Tyndale House Publishers.

9. Alert and Ready: Lessons from Laodicea

1. Barton, B., Comfort, P., Osborne, G., Taylor, L. K., & Veerman, D. (2001). *Life Application New Testament Commentary* (p. 1218). Wheaton, IL: Tyndale.

10. The Absolute Authority of the Bible

1. When the Bible speaks of an abundant life the primary focus is not materialistic. The idea of an abundant life is first a spiritually abundant life. God wants us to thrive spiritually. God will quickly sacrifice our material wealth and possessions to move us to a higher place spiritually.

11. A Biblical Theology of Suffering

1. God did not stop Adam and Eve from sinning even though He could have. He allowed them to choose what they wanted to do. It is amazing that God permitted Adam and Eve to sin against Him, as not only did it affect humanity, but it also affected Him negatively. Now, even God was going to also experience sin and death.
2. This begs the question. Why should we suffer for what Adam and Eve did? The short answer is this. Should God afford each of us the same opportunity as Adam and Eve, we would each make the same decisions. Therefore, for this reason we are all guilty in Adam and Eve.

12. The Fear of the Lord

1. Source: CS Lewis, *The Lion, the Witch & The Wardrobe* (Penguin, 1950)
2. The definition of idolatry here is any understanding or belief that minimizes the nature, character, and attributes of God, i.e., any idea that makes God less than the God of the Bible.
3. God is the unfathomable Mystery before whom we are awestruck and stand trembling, yet find ourselves inexorably drawn into relationship, attracted, and fascinated in ways we cannot fully explain.
4. http://www.saintstephenlutheran.net/2011/05/fearing-god/
5. The Pursuit of God and Other Classics, by A.W. Tozer, Christian Publications, Inc. Harrisburg, Pa.
6. https://www.sermoncentral.com/sermon-illustrations/68891/one-time-many-years-ago-the-king-of-hungary-by-ajai-prakash
7. It is strange many Christians today have an aversion to the idea of punishment, especially in relationship to God. They say it sounds so harsh and mean. Even in public gatherings the word is avoided. However, over 170 times the word punishment or its derivatives are used in the scriptures, while at the same time the word forgiveness and its derivatives are used a little over 140 times. Why are we so quick to point out God's forgiveness, but ignore the fact that He does punish?
8. Notice that Job completely ignores Satan. Job realizes that Satan is not responsible for what is happening to him. He knows who is in charge and who is responsible.
9. To question God's integrity is completely out of order. How can the clay say to the potter, "What are you doing?"
10. Sin or unrighteous as defined by God and not by culture or self. If God is not okay with it, then we as followers of Christ cannot be okay with it.
11. (from Keil and Delitzsch Commentary on the Old Testament: New Updated Edition, Electronic Database. Copyright © 1996 by Hendrickson Publishers, Inc. All rights reserved.)
12. bereanresearch.org/**whatever-happened-fear-lord**/ It was posted by Marsha West on August 16, 2016 in Biblical Illiteracy, Discernment 30.
13. http://www.christianitytoday.com/biblestudies/bible-answers/spirituallife/what-does-it-mean-to-fear-god.html

13. The Problem of Sin

1. (from Adam Clarke's Commentary, Electronic Database. Copyright © 1996, 2003, 2005, 2006 by Biblesoft, Inc. All rights reserved.)
2. *The Prairie Overcomer*

14. Eternal Punishment

1. There was question as to its duration and whether after a time there was annihilation. However, this was later cleared up by the further teachings of Jesus and the other New Testament writers.
2. There is a false idea that God does not send people to hell, but people choose hell. This thought avoids the idea of a loving God sending someone to hell as a punishment.

Made in the USA
Monee, IL
16 May 2022